NAKED AT THE ALBERT HALL

THE INSIDE STORY OF SINGING

TRACEY THORN

virago

VIRAGO

First published in Great Britain in 2015 by Virago Press
This paperback edition published in 2016 by Virago Press

1 3 5 7 9 10 8 6 4 2

A CIP catalogue record for this book
is available from the British Library.

ISBN 978-0-349-00524-9

Typeset in Bembo by M Rules
Printed and bound in Great Britain by
Clays Ltd, St Ives plc

Papers used by Virago are from well-managed forests
and other responsible sources.

Tracey Thorn was singer and songwriter with Everything But the Girl from 1982–2000. At that point she semi-retired from the music business to bring up her children. She has since recorded three solo albums, *Out of the Woods*, *Love and Its Opposite* and *Tinsel and Lights*, and published her bestselling autobiography, *Bedsit Disco Queen*. She lives in London with her husband Ben Watt and their three children.

'Smart, chatty ... [Thorn is] a sufficiently deft writer to negotiate the populist and the high-brow ... a thought-provoking and enjoyable read' *Mail on Sunday*

'Honest and compassionate' *Sunday Telegraph*

'If you care at all about pop music you should read both [*Naked at the Albert Hall* and *Bedsit Disco Queen*]' *Sunday Herald*

'Revelatory, always entertaining ... a genuine insider's perspective ... Thirty years of consideration went into this quietly impressive volume, and it shows' *Independent*

'A writer in fine voice ... [a] cracker of a book' *Scotsman*

'Thorn is the perfect analyst of our reverence for and terror of singing ... Thorn's practical, warm tone gives her a Miss Marple-like ability to appear kindly while holding mistruths up to account ... She is best, though, as a sympathetic guide to the singers she loves' *Daily Telegraph*

'Tracey's characterful phrasing is as persuasive on page as it is on record' *Grazia*

'Gem-like confessions that make it feel like a proper discussion. I loved it' Nina Stibbe, *Telegraph*

By Tracey Thorn

Bedsit Disco Queen
Naked at the Albert Hall

FOREWORD

We love singing, don't we? Both doing it and listening to it. We sing when we're happy and celebrating – 'Happy Birthday to You' – and we sing when we're down, in an attempt to keep our spirits up. We sing when we're bored, to try and make the time pass faster – silly songs on coach trips, repetitive songs on long walks. Like whistling in the dark, we all sing together sometimes when we're afraid, soldiers marching in unison to 'It's a Long Way to Tipperary'; and we choose songs to make light of things that are unutterably gloomy – I'm reminded of the end of the film *The Inn of the Sixth Happiness*, when Gladys Aylward (Ingrid Bergman) leads her orphans over the mountains and to safety, all bravely singing, 'This old man, he played one, he played knick-knack on my thumb . . . '

We sing to elevate sporting events – 'Abide with Me', 'Swing Low, Sweet Chariot'; we sing when we're winning – 'We're on our way to Wembley'; and when we're

losing, others remark on our silence by singing themselves – 'You're not singing any more'. We sing all together
on the dancefloor, even if you can't hear us, and after a few
drinks we'll get up with a karaoke microphone and sing so
you *can* hear us. At big concerts we sing along en masse,
and we like nothing better than being given the chance to
join in a call-and-response with our heroes on stage, echoing them, copying phrases they give us.

We sing at serious occasions, too; in church, at weddings,
christenings, funerals. We form choirs, to sing either hymns
and classical pieces, or vocal arrangements of rock songs.
We're encouraged nowadays to join in, whether or not we
feel we can 'really sing'. It's good for us, apparently; a
recently published piece of research suggests that, like med-
itation, singing has a relaxing effect on the body, lowering
blood pressure and thus helping us along the path to a
longer, healthier life. Another study claims that singing
exercises could strengthen the throat muscles and somehow
ease snoring. And it's 'good' for us too: morally uplifting,
an improving activity. Classical music has been linked with
ideas of morality since the eighteenth century, and the
teaching of singing became at least in part an exercise in
fostering good behaviour. 'Music as morality and singing as
discipline were at the very root of Victorian church music',
writes John Potter in his book *Vocal Authority*, and singing
became an important part of infant school education.
Along with jam-making, the Women's Institute became
famous for its communal singing of 'Jerusalem' at meetings.
A bit self-important, a bit goody-goody, it was what put my
mum off for life the first time she went. Unable to take

seriously the sight of a group of housewives solemnly intoning William Blake's hymn, she got a fit of the giggles, and never returned.

And yet, despite the fact that we do it all the time, when people are asked what talent they would most like to have, they often answer that they wish they could sing. It's a shared dream, a fantasy talent. A skill, like being able to speak another language, or paint, which we feel would free us, define us, make us more entertaining and interesting, and more able to express ourselves. We elevate singing above many other activities, often endowing it with an almost religious significance, and believe that both in singing, and in listening to others sing, we can experience something transcendent. So we mythologise and romanticise singing and singers, seeming to hold it up as a skill both more difficult and rarer than it actually is – talent show auditions reveal that in fact quite a lot of people can sing; it's not as unique as we tend to assume. This elevation of singing is a romantic notion, and can be flattering – if you happen to be a singer – yet also strangely reductive. When we regard singing as an instinctive and wholly emotional act, we narrow down our understanding of what it is and what singers are. If we think of it as simply a primal out-pouring of feeling, then we miss the elements of conscious control and decision-making that go into singing, and which can make the difference between boring singing and interesting singing. I don't mean to deny the emotional aspect, but what I do often find myself pointing out is: there's more thinking in singing than you might think.

*

These are the thoughts that have led me to write this book. It's not intended to be Part Two of my memoir, *Bedsit Disco Queen*, in which I described much of my career in music, but it is connected. In writing an autobiography there is inevitably a certain amount that gets left out. You have to settle on a tone of voice, and a stance, in order to avoid merely compiling a long list of things that happened; and with *Bedsit Disco Queen*, my chosen stance was all to do with my attempts to make myself fit in a world – the music business – which I more or less stumbled into. It was a book about ambivalence, and the quest for personal identity; about love of music and awkwardness with music; about fame and strangeness and the attempt to cling to some kind of normality. What it wasn't, particularly, was a book about being a singer, and after I'd written it some people asked me why I hadn't said much about singing – in places skating over the very aspect of my life that has publicly defined me, and often referring only in passing to how I feel about singing and what it means to me. I left certain details out, because I wanted to write a book that was pacy, and funny, and kept moving forward, and had moments of introspection without getting bogged down in them. But having written that book, I feel that I can step back and slow down, and take a longer look at some of the thoughts that I filed away in a corner of my mind, hoping to come back to them later. Some of the things I want to say in this book are almost footnotes to *Bedsit Disco Queen*, or digressions on subjects that it briefly alighted on. Conversations that I half started, or alluded to, but raced past without finishing. Or thoughts that only occurred to me later.

This book might seem personal and idiosyncratic, but that's because it's not a journalist's investigative exploration of the story of singing, or an academic's all-inclusive encyclopedia. It's more a compendium of insights which I haven't often seen recorded or discussed; alternative takes on aspects of singing which are taken for granted. The fact, for instance, that as the person doing the singing, you can drift towards feeling resentful of the idea that you are simply in possession of a natural gift, and that there is an artlessness to the occupation you are known for. Singing is a physical activity as much as an emotional one, and though the sound is produced in the very core of your body – from the lungs, right next to the heart – the brain is always involved too. Decisions are being made all the time, ones which require attention and focus – settling on the range in which you're going to sing, which part of your voice you're going to use, your pronunciation, accent, inflection, sense of rhythm, volume, dynamics ... These are constants – ongoing operational decisions which may feel instinctive, or become second nature through practice and habit, but which are nonetheless mental and intellectual activities, not simply happy accidents. There are technical choices, too, involving microphones and headphones, setting up volume and balance, and moving in and out from the microphone to alter the sound. All these things have an effect on performance. And the question of 'taste' – not only in what songs to sing, but *how* to sing them – brings an aesthetic consciousness to the process of singing. Again, this is a mental process, not a mere outrush of emotion.

I don't often hear people say these kinds of things about singing, so this book will, in part, be an insider's view, an uncovering of secrets about singing, things that are known only to those who have sung for their supper. However, since I'm writing from both sides of the fence, as a listener as well as a singer, I want to include my point of view as an enthusiast, talking about voices I love, trying to get inside them. I'm writing as a book-lover, too, drawn to those points where my love of singing and my love of literature overlap; where novels or poems articulate deeper truths about singing, and its significance. There are characters in fiction who embody different aspects of the singer's role and life, and I want to look at them as a way of exploring the singer as a symbol, as well as a living, breathing human being.

With all these goals, and my wish to hang onto a very personal viewpoint, I'm aware that this book will be neither chronological, like a memoir, nor will it follow the arc of an argument. I have no particular point to prove, or specific conclusion to reach. I plan to follow stories that particularly interest me, wherever they may lead; sometimes one idea may lead to another, sometimes a new train of thought might interpose itself. There'll be a playful element to some of it, as I make what might seem to be fanciful connections between apparently unlikely things: a lyric by The Streets leading me to a poem by Siegfried Sassoon, or a Franz Kafka short story making me think of Vashti Bunyan.

But I will also talk about my own singing and how I feel about it; about books and talent shows, microphones and

Auto-Tune; about the debate between artifice and authenticity. I will ask a few other singers what *they* think, and try to work out what it is we want from them – and whether it is anything they can possibly provide. When we talk or write about singers, what do we say? And how much do we really understand what it feels like to be a singer? We love listening to singers, and sometimes we dream of being one ourselves, so we assume that it must be an uncomplicated source of fulfilment and joy to sing for a living. And yet, having been a singer for most of my adult life, and having read many biographies of singers I love, I'm all too aware that this isn't always the case; that singers can be bundles of neuroses, tormented by anxiety about their vocal inadequacy, fears about losing their voice, about it failing them – or, equally, about it defining them too much, at the cost of their personality. Being loved for your voice can be great, but it leads to the question: does anybody love me for myself?

For you may feel that you're nothing special. That in fact, you're a bit of a bore. And it may be that, if you tell a joke, we've probably heard it before. But if you have a talent, and everyone listens when you start to sing, is that really nothing more complicated than 'a wonderful thing'? Or is it perhaps more of a mixed blessing, and one that should come with a clear warning sign: 'This way danger lies'?

A HANDFUL OF NOTES

I don't do nostalgia gigs. And by that, I don't just mean I don't perform them, I mean I don't attend them either. I don't believe in them. I really don't want them. For one thing, they make me feel old in a way that it is wholly unhelpful and destructive. I don't mind being the age I am – I've reached a level of achievement I'm happy with, I enjoy my daily routines, I feel comfortable in my own skin. I don't long to be eighteen again, or twenty-five, and it was between those ages that I experienced most of my gig-going high points. So going to a gig to watch a band I loved years back, playing an album I loved at the time, just seems masochistic – nothing more than an exercise in pointing out to yourself that it was all a long time ago, that *they're* old and *we're* old, and all of it is over. Which isn't really what I believe. The great things about that record you loved, they're not over. You carry them with you, they've shaped you, they're part of you. As my old friend Peter Walsh, from Australian group The Apartments, never tires of quoting at me, 'The past isn't dead. It isn't even past' (William Faulkner), and this is precisely why I don't feel any need to have my nose rubbed in a musical history which has never really left me.

And yet. Here I am, it's June 2005, and I'm in a seat at the Royal Festival Hall. I've broken my own rule and come to a nostalgia gig, a performance of a seminal album. I've bought the ticket and I'm here, and now, in truth, I'm excited, getting in the mood. It won't be as bad as you fear, I reassure myself. Come on, it might be good, you might enjoy it. Relax.

The lights dim. Onto the stage walks the singer. She's wearing the jacket from the cover of the album, and that's good. She looks older, sure, unashamedly older, and that's good too. Of all people I would have hated *her* to buy into a desperate chasing of eternal youth – nipping here, tucking there. Now she's appeared I'm feeling a frisson of proper excitement. Maybe I'm going to be completely won over after all. The piano line starts up – and yes, it's true, it sounds exactly right. In she comes, with that opening line, maybe the best opening line ever, and suddenly – without me even knowing how I got out of my seat – I'm on my feet, my arms are in the air, I think there may even be tears in my eyes. And more than that, I'm transported, I'm whirling through the air, through time and space, and I'm back in my little orange-painted bedroom at home, and I'm tipping the album out of its sleeve and slipping it onto the spindle of the blue Dansette I inherited from my brother, and she's singing that opening line. And the line is . . . And the line is . . .

'Jesus died for somebody's sins, but not mine.'

When did you know you could sing? people ask me. How did you even start? Where does your voice come from, is it from inside your head or inside your body? It's not like other musical instruments, is it, and because of this there are aspects of what we sound like which will be for ever out of our control. The moment when we first encounter the sound that comes out of our own body can be a profound and decisive one. I've written before that it was a disappointment to me when I realised I wouldn't be Patti Smith, but that was a little way off in the future when I first heard her in 1979. The introduction was made by Mike Harris from down the road, who'd lent me her album *Horses*, along with Stiff Records' *The Akron Compilation* in a scratch 'n' sniff sleeve smelling of rubber. My first reaction to Patti was one of possibility. I wanted to be her because a) on the cover of the record she looked like a boy, and I felt that I pretty much looked like a boy, and she made looking like a boy seem a beautiful thing; and b) the first time I tried to sing along with those opening lines on *Horses*, I realised in fact that I *could* sound like her. I was sixteen, the idea of singing had barely entered my head, and yet somewhere inside me vague imaginings, unformed desires, were beginning to stir and take shape.

That record's opening lines, from her version of 'Gloria', have now passed into rock mythology, but I can still recall the visceral jolt of hearing them for the first time. And not just the audacity of the words, the defiant sneer, but the tone of the voice – worldly, dismissive – and beyond even that, the pitch of the voice. Low, dark, boyish, it existed in a space that seemed familiar, and contained echoes of the sound I was tentatively exploring in the privacy of my bedroom. Joining in with her I found that we did indeed occupy the same ground, and without knowing how or why I had an immediate sense of my voice 'fitting'. Imagining this to be an entirely conceptual 'fit', I of course believed that I sounded a bit like Patti Smith because we *were* alike, it was a metaphysical connection being made. And in doing so I fell into the first and most basic misconception about vocal influence and inspiration – the idea that it transcends the physical. Now, I believe that the reason she implanted herself into my imagination as my first vocal influence was the simple accident of vocal range; the fact that in that first song I heard her sing, 'Gloria', she comes in on a low E, the E below middle C, and for the rest of the song moves around within the space between this E and the one an octave above. My perfect, ideal range. Still the place I most like to sing.

I'd sung along with pop records before, of course I had. But never before had one demonstrated to me the perfect place for my voice to be. So when I talk about my lack of stage presence and self-confidence, and in doing so imply there's something almost ridiculous in my wanting to be Patti Smith, maybe I'm in danger of forgetting this ultimate truth – that at the very moment I was beginning to experiment with the idea of singing, I heard a singer embodying in one six-minute song a version of myself both simplified – a black and white version with no grey areas – and amplified.

Almost the entire *Horses* album is pitched perfectly for me, as I discovered during the evenings that followed this epiphany. My parents would take the dog out for a daily walk, leaving me with fifteen luxurious minutes of solitude in which I would sing along at full volume with various tracks. 'Kimberly', for instance, with its melody that lingers and hovers around the note B, slap bang in the middle of my range, where my voice is at its strongest and fullest. Joining in with Patti on these songs was a joyous experience, utterly secret, something I shared with nobody. The basic physical coincidence of our vocal ranges connected us not just ideologically, but physiologically.

If you talk about the voice as being a musical instrument, you can make it sound like something tangible. In his book *Vocal Authority*, John Potter describes it, in mechanical terms, as being made up of three elements: 'a power supply (the lungs), an oscillator (the cords, or vocal folds as they are sometimes called), and a resonator (the vocal tract, consisting of the mouth and throat cavities)'. The lungs propel air, which passes through the vocal cords, making them vibrate and producing the sound we use for either speaking or singing. But unlike any other instrument, these components are your own actual body parts, and the sound you make is both defined and limited by your anatomy. As an instrumentalist you might practise and adapt your technique in order to follow the style and sound of players you like, and you might then call this influence. But as a singer there is only so much you can ever do to adapt the sound of your voice to emulate other singers. We label as inspirational those singers we happen to sound like. We feel a kinship with those whose sound lives somewhere close to our own, or at least seems to come from a similar neighbourhood.

It's also true that we can be negatively influenced by people, or strain to avoid taking on too strongly the imprint of another, for fear of drifting into mere imitation and un-originality. Bob Dylan talks in his book, *Chronicles*, about how intimidated he could be in the early days by hearing others who seemed more authentic than him, and how inadequate that could make him feel. He'd been learning and playing all of Woody Guthrie's songs, and feeling pretty good about himself as a singer of these songs, when he suddenly heard the recordings of Ramblin' Jack Elliott, who'd been singing the same songs for years. Dylan describes being devastated by this – 'I felt like I'd been cast into sudden hell'. Far from being inspired by the sound of someone doing what he was trying to do, he felt paralysed, and realised that in fact he would have to run a million miles from the very person it seemed he could learn the most from. All he could do was try to ignore Elliott – 'It would be hard not to be influenced by the guy I just heard. I'd have to block it out of my mind . . . tell myself I hadn't heard him and he didn't exist.' In other words, influence can sometimes be terrifying – not inspiring at all, but crippling.

When I started, it was more often male singers with whom I connected – Elvis Costello and I shared a lot of range – and a little while later the dark brown tones of

Nico's singing provided another source of influence, or inspiration. In perhaps my favourite line from his recent *Autobiography*, Morrissey describes Nico thus: 'Her singing voice is the sound of a body falling downstairs.' Certainly there's a downward trajectory to her singing, which reflected my own vocal style. In an early interview with *Melody Maker*, it was pointed out to me that I must have been influenced by Bridget St John, who in all honesty I had never heard of. Learning that she was a folk singer from the early 1970s, I took umbrage at the comparison and made a conscious effort to avoid finding out anything more about her. Years – no, truthfully, decades – later, I did investigate, and discovered that the distance from her *Ask Me No Questions* album to my *A Distant Shore* is only a few short steps. Vocally we are kin. Lyrically we are kin. She must have loved Nico, too, so maybe we both simply took some cues from the same place, but it's fascinating to come across the singers whom you seem to have been magically influenced by without ever having heard them.

My range was tiny at first; on the earliest recordings I made, with the Marine Girls, I sang only a handful of notes. By the time I came to make *A Distant Shore* in 1981, only a couple of years after hearing Patti Smith and getting an inkling that I might want to sing, I still hadn't really learned how to do it properly, so there are moments where it gets a bit 'pitchy' – to use modern parlance – but that's counterbalanced by the complete absorption of the performance. It's the record where I began to find out for myself what I might sound like, or be able to sound like, and there's a sensuality to the vocal which is the result of finally having the mic to myself and simply revelling in the experience – all that lovely reverb, all that lovely low vibrato, God I was enjoying myself! I can remember the freedom of the experience; I was on my own for the first time, without the other Marine Girls, and I sang without the inhibition I sometimes felt in their presence. In front of them, I was wary of 'showing off', of implying that my singing was better than Alice's, of indulging myself. But here I was able to admit to myself that I *could* sing, and so something of my own style and vocal personality was unlocked; the voice that would be recognisably mine came out into the open and declared itself. But whether I found that voice, or invented it, is a question that has always mystified and intrigued me.

It was in many ways a small voice, but it was all mine, and for years I didn't try very hard to do much with it, either to extend or improve it. My approach was that of the passionate amateur, grateful to find myself in possession of a talent that others valued, never exploring much further beyond the realms of what came easily, or 'naturally'. Singing live and touring meant that I had to try to sing louder, and build up some endurance, but other than that I remained faithful to the handful of notes which constituted my sound. I couldn't go very high and it didn't really occur to me to try, until around 1989 when I began to experiment with my higher head voice, or falsetto, you might call it. I hadn't ever wanted to use it before, it didn't sound like 'me', and it was startling to hear myself sing outside my range. I used it intermittently from the Everything But The Girl album *Worldwide* onwards, but only grew into it in a comfortable sense during my resurrected solo career after 2007. My producer Ewan Pearson and I joked during the recording of *Out of the Woods* and *Love and Its Opposite* that on those two records I sang the highest notes I had ever reached for in my entire life – these being the highest harmony on 'don't tell me it's too late' at the end of 'Raise the Roof', and the 'sun in your hair' line in the middle of 'Kentish Town'. I needed stepladders to reach them.

It was a very long way from Patti Smith, and not the voice I'd found when I first tried to sing. It must have been there all the time, but hidden away – it needed me to locate it, and then to believe that it sounded OK and have the confidence to use it, before I finally added this bit of range to the notes I had available. I thought that my identity was moored for ever in those first few notes I sang – and to some extent I will always think of that part of my voice as the real me – but still, I've learned that although range is both natural and instinctive, it can also involve an element of choice; that extra range can be uncovered, or released, or simply willed into being. These notes, they all come out of the same body, the source of all the sound we make.

2

TISSUE AND SKIN AND BONE

If the sound we make is at least in part determined by anatomy, then which parts, I wonder, might influence the way I sing, and contribute to the way I naturally sound? I'd imagine that strong lungs, an open, relaxed throat and a sense of ease and control in the mouth and jaw would be essential for a singer, or would at least contribute to successful singing. But when I examine myself and my physical history, I realise that I don't meet these requirements, and that limitations have played a part in the development of my singing and some of the problems I have with it.

First off, I've always had weak lungs. Due to an accident at birth, I inhaled fluid and developed pneumonia as a consequence, not a good start for baby lungs. As a child I had a chesty, loose, smoker's cough every winter, which my mum would dose up with Phensedyl, a medicine which at that time you could buy over the counter but which doctors gradually became more strict about prescribing. She came home one day from the chemist saying she had had to sign the poison book in order to get a new bottle for me, because apparently the local junkies were drinking it on the village green. At that age I had no idea why, though I found out some years later when I glugged back too much of it in a hotel room in Germany while coughing my way through a tour, and spent a hallucinatory afternoon in bed listening to the kettle in the corner of the room talking to me. In my twenties I developed asthma as a result of living with two cats I turned out to be allergic to, and so asthma inhalers were added to the chest complaints section of my medicine cupboard.

The anatomy of the throat – the way in which the larynx and vocal cords are put together – must obviously play a part, too. I had to go for a laryngoscopy a couple of years ago when a small operation, for which I'd required a general anaesthetic, revealed some difficulty during the anaesthetising procedure, possibly an obstruction in my throat. The doctor recommended I get it checked out. This was terrifying, both medically (oh my God an obstruction in my throat obviously a tumour I am dead) and musically (could I have developed some problem with my larynx or vocal cords – polyps, nodules – which might put an end to my singing?). With my throat numbed, the specialist inserted a tiny camera up my nose and down into my throat, declaring within a few minutes that all was normal, and that this was just bloody typical of anaesthetists who, if they ever had a difficult intubation, would immediately refer the patient to a throat specialist, arguing there must be some anatomical problem. Apparently this time there wasn't – my throat was fine. After all those years of singing, it was the first time anyone had looked at it, so it was a relief to hear this.

And what about the anatomy of the mouth and jaw? Here, too, I have encountered problems, a deviation from what's considered 'normal'. When I was a child my dentist noticed that I was developing a pronounced underbite, meaning that my teeth didn't meet well. He wanted to perform surgery, essentially carving a section out of my lower jawbone and reconstructing my entire jaw, so that my teeth would meet nicely. Mum refused to even countenance the procedure, much to my relief, and it was never mentioned again. Years later, in my twenties, probably, a different dentist asked if I'd ever considered having anything done about my malocclusion. I told him about the suggested childhood operation and he whistled through his teeth. 'Thank God your mother didn't agree to that,' he said. 'Brutal. We don't do *that* nowadays.' Then he went on to describe the current procedure – a simple case of having my jaw broken and re-set. OK, I said, and why would I want to have that done? Well, he said, you'd look different. I didn't know if I wanted to look different. Would I *sound* different? I asked. He wasn't sure. I was, however, sure I didn't want to sound different. He told me it would be best to have it done before a certain age – thirty-something, was it? I forget now. I went home and let the years drift by until it was hopefully past the point of being possible.

But I can only assume that it all contributes, that every bit of the anatomy involved in producing sound must have an impact on the final quality of that sound. Classical singer

Ian Bostridge is the author of a fascinating book called *A Singer's Notebook*, in which he describes going to a singing teacher who works with a laryngologist and a physiotherapist to concentrate on the mechanical aspects of singing. He observes: 'My teacher's most interesting general point about the vocal mechanism is that, unlike the piano, it is not designed for the purpose with which we most associate it. The primary function of the vocal tract is as one of several lines of defence against choking ... If I've understood him properly, much of what we do as singers, particularly in achieving the high notes that technique facilitates, is actually about persuading the body that one is not about to swallow as one reaches for the skies.'

I love this fact: that, as singers, we are not only working with a mechanism inside our own bodies, but a mechanism that isn't even really intended to do what we try to make it do. Every effort to produce a beautiful sound is an effort to overcome the limitations of our apparatus. It's like trying to use a cheese grater or a vacuum cleaner to make music, and doesn't this make singing seem both mundane and heroic?

The idea that there might be something remarkable about the physiology of the singer, especially the classical singer, is one that recurs in literature. In Willa Cather's 1915 novel *The Song of the Lark*, there is a scene where the singer and protagonist Thea Kronborg is examined physically, her teacher feeling her larynx while she breathes and sings, and she is described as being designed to be a singer – 'the big mouth, the wide jaw and chin, the strong white teeth, the deep laugh. The machine was so simple and strong, seemed to be so easily operated. She sang from the bottom of her-self.'

And again in George du Maurier's bestselling novel *Trilby*, when Svengali meets the singer Trilby he examines her like a breeder checking out a racehorse, peering into her open mouth and declaring, 'The roof of your mouth is like the dome of the Pantheon ... The entrance to your throat is like the middle porch of St Sulpice ... and the bridge of your nose is like the belly of a Stradivarius – what a sounding board! And inside your beautiful big chest the lungs are made of leather!' These descriptions are strikingly architectural and mechanical in their language, as though the singer's body is a building or a machine – the grander the cathedral, the stronger the machine, the bigger and better the voice. Similarly, in his book about opera and homosexuality, *The Queen's Throat*, Wayne Koestenbaum talks about Maria Callas: 'Walter Legge, who produced many of Callas's legendary recordings, once peered inside her mouth and remarked that it was shaped like a Gothic cathedral.'

It's as if there is something out of the ordinary, then, about the mouths and throats of singers. As a singer, it could make you self-conscious to dwell on this thought, and that is the last thing you need; you become very aware of your body, more so than other musicians. While I'm very wary of risking sounding like a comedy mime artist – MY BODY IS MY TOOL – it is a simple truth that unlike other musicians, who use an instrument made of wood, strings, brass or electronic components to make their sound, we have to use something made of tissue, skin and bone. Musicians are famous for the care they take of their instruments – buying first-class airline seats for expensive cellos, for instance, or keeping guitar collections in temperature- and humidity-controlled environments – but for singers the equivalent is to lavish fastidious care on the body itself, to a degree which can become tiresome and restrictive. Classical singers take it for granted that rest and quiet are an essential part of touring, whiling away their days gently cosseting their voices and indulging in anxieties and neuroses which are seen as a natural and serious part of their job. The rock singer is supposed to be above all this, to devote more energy to shouting, drinking and hotel-trashing, but it is an unacknowledged fact that not all singers outside the classical realm can afford to play fast and loose with their voices in a Led Zeppelin-like manner. The amplified rock/pop voice can be as hard to maintain, requiring similarly dull regimes of conversation-avoidance, herbal teas and early nights. The anxieties induced by colds and upper respiratory tract infections mean that singers can become preoccupied by the state of the ear, nose and throat areas, and the presence or otherwise of that basic bodily substance, phlegm. Phlegm is an absolute nuisance to the singer, present – as for most people – in greater quantities in the morning, and makes early performances, for instance on breakfast TV shows, something of a throat-clearing nightmare, to be avoided whenever possible. Eating also causes phlegm to be produced, and so meals before a gig are troublesome. On tour, the structure of the day usually means that arrival at the venue will be followed by a soundcheck, leaving an hour or two before the show in which to eat and get ready. But that is already too close to showtime to eat a meal, and so often – like many singers, I suspect – I would choose not to eat much at this time of the day. Later, there would be sandwiches at the hotel, or a bumper bag of crisps on the tour bus; no proper food, no fruit or vegetables. And then we wonder why we fall prey to colds and respiratory tract infections.

Recently I asked Romy Madley Croft, singer with the xx, about being on tour, and was relieved when it transpired that she was the same as me – perhaps the same as all of us singers. 'I used to struggle with constantly having a sore throat on tour,' she said. 'This might be too much information but I realised it came from exposure to lots of air conditioning, getting a blocked nose and that leading to me breathing through my mouth when I slept, giving me a dry throat. My only singing-on-tour tip is taking decongestant spray with me.' See? We're all frustrated ear, nose and throat specialists.

Talking can become a problem, too, especially if, as I believe many people do, you talk less from the diaphragm, like Shakespearean actors, and more from the throat. A lot of talking can tire and strain the voice, yet tours are often accompanied by non-stop promotional activities and interviews. I have always found speaking on the phone especially problematic – something about the fact of not being able to see the other person forces you into a greater degree of voice projection and tension. An afternoon of face-to-face or phone interviews could be disastrous, and eventually these were things I backed away from. At times when my voice was really struggling, I would avoid all talking, spending the day solitary and silent, reading and looking out of the window, nursing medicinal teas, pacing wordlessly in the dressing room rather than socialising and enjoying the build-up to a gig.

All these physical issues are impossible to suppress completely; they just have to be worked around. And they ensure that singers are neurotic about certain tiny aspects of their physiology. As Ian Bostridge writes, 'It makes us . . . a very inward-looking breed, literally, obsessed with the health of tiny pieces of mucous membrane (the vocal cords) in the cartilaginous larynx . . . ' But this basic fact – that the voice is a body, or at least, inhabits a body, and is produced physically, via the movement of muscles, air passing over the larynx and so on – is also what connects singers to their audience, in a way that is different from other musicians. In his brilliant book, *Performing Rites*, the critic and sociomusicologist Simon Frith points out that as the audience we are aware, consciously or not, that we too possess the same physical attributes – lungs, larynx, vocal cords. When we listen to music we can't usually *play* along, but we can and do sing along. We have the same body as the singers we are listening to, we come tantalisingly close to being able to do what they can do, and so the very body which makes the singer so neurotic is also what bonds her to the audience. All of us make sounds all the time – we speak, we laugh, we cry – but if we are not musicians we may never go near a musical instrument, never use one to make a sound with. Musicians, therefore, are separate, distinct from us, in a way that singers are not. Still, singers reveal to us that they can do more with the body than we can, and so they are us, but better. We see ourselves not only reflected, but enhanced, improved upon. The bond is at once egalitarian yet also hierarchical – we identify with and we revere singers – and there, in a nutshell, is the source of some of their power over us.

3

A WONDERFUL TOY

The voice is not just a body, however, it's also a person, and this, too, makes it quite unlike other musical instruments. We usually identify more with singers than other musicians, and we identify them more completely with their songs. In *Performing Rites*, Simon Frith writes about the fact that we regard vocal expression as being more direct than when a musician expresses themselves via a guitar or drum kit. Despite it being a performance, containing elements of imagination, acting and projection, we often take singing very literally, imagining that what we hear or think we hear is a direct and faithful expression of the singer's personal feelings or their personality. We feel we get to know singers by listening to them sing, and if we like the voice, we tend to imagine that we like the person.

I have a confession to make: when I listen to bands, I only really hear the singer.

People say, 'Great bass line on that track,' or 'LOVE the drummer in that band,' and as a teenager, when I was starting to buy records and take them seriously, I simply didn't know what they were talking about. I was unable to identify what the bass player was doing, or understand what his or her role was. Drumming was more obvious – you couldn't not hear it, after all – but still, for me it was going on in the background. As for the other instruments, well, they were there to hold the tune together and move it along, to weave a kind of aural net, the purpose of which was to bear the singer aloft and carry them towards you so that they could deliver the true purpose of the music – the lead vocal.

Joining a band provided a brisk Dummies' Guide to Instruments, and I began to understand what each member was doing. I learned how to join in with the conversation, and trained myself to pay attention to the other things that were going on apart from the singer. But that didn't mean I ever quite moved on from my earliest perception, and even now I don't think I hear music that differently. This leads me to wonder, is it possible to like a band, or any record, if you don't like the singer? Is my way of listening really so unusual, or is it the way most of us hear music?

It can even be difficult to like a band if you have reservations about the singer, or get stuck on some mannerism or other. I've always found it hard to get past that whistling sibilance on every 's' that Damon Albarn pronounces, and it stood in the way of me ever having any real affection for Blur. On his more recent projects, some of the intonations and glottal stops have been dialled down, but still, that 's' is a funny little tic. It's out of his control, obviously, and mean of me to mention it, but on just such minor and apparently trivial points can our feelings about singers snag.

On the other hand, it's possible to like the singer but not the band. In the Oasis/Blur wars I was on the wrong side, in that I favoured Oasis. Everything they subsequently went on to become, which was hinted at right from the beginning – repetitive, retrogressive, lumpen – versus everything that Blur went on to become – imaginative, open-minded – should have made it obvious who was better. But I had a simple singer preference. On those early singles, Liam Gallagher's singing was spectacular – a sneering engine of a voice levelled straight at your forehead, the first vocalist since John Lydon to capture that underdog spirit of defiance in all its glory. 'I'm feeling supersonic/GIVE me gin and tonic' he demanded, not even bothering to take his hands out of his pockets. At the super-slick, stage-managed MTV Awards I attended in New York he rolled on to the stage, spat on the floor, sang at us with lazy, contemptuous fury, and made me feel proud to be British. But his voice really was the most impressive thing about them, and once I'd had a few blasts of it via the first three or four singles, I felt I'd really had the best of them.

It reminded me, though, that the singer is almost always the way in to the band. It's both a pro and a con of being a singer; audiences feel close and connected to you, and you can reach your listeners in a way that instrumentalists have to strive harder to do. On the other hand, someone *not* liking your voice can feel very much like them not liking *you*. As well as concern for one's physical well-being that can border on the neurotic, the unavoidably personal element can add to a singer's sensitivity and self-consciousness; the sense that singing is an exposing thing to do, or at least that an audience, and critics, interpret it as such, and consider themselves entitled to make judgements which, when negative, can feel like attacks on the person.

But a positive judgement can turn into something else entirely: an unrealistic and idealised version of the person doing the singing. It's not a new phenomenon – Simon Frith discusses the idea of the star singer originating in classical music, before it was adopted by the world of pop: 'The mass cultural notion of stardom, combining a Romantic belief in genius with a promise to make it individually available as a commodity ... derives as much from the packaging of "high" artists as from the hype of the low'. In the early nineteenth century, for instance, the Swedish soprano Jenny Lind went on a US tour, which was masterminded by P. T. Barnum, and sold extensive merchandising. What we'd now call a marketing strategy was created around her, which emphasised her virginal innocence, her spiritual purity, her 'authenticity'. She was presented as something superhuman but also unreal, sanitised, infantilised; she was more than just a woman singing a song, she was an Ideal, a Symbol. And perhaps this desire to deify the singer, to stress her purity and goodness, reflected something prevalent at that time, namely an anxiety about the moral status of singing, the probity of performance, of The Stage.

This idea is explored in George Eliot's *Daniel Deronda*, written in 1876, a book which is full of characters who sing, and who fret over what singing says about them, how it reflects upon them as citizens, where it places them in society. Daniel Deronda himself has had a good singing voice since he was a boy – one of those angelic, choirboy voices 'which seem to bring an idyllic heaven and earth before our eyes'. Anxious about his social standing – he does not know who his parents are and has been brought up by the uncle he secretly believes to be his father – he is alert to any indication of a slight concerning his social status. When his uncle suggests to him as a boy that he could become a professional singer, he is horrified, and replies angrily, 'No; I should hate it!' Daniel has a clear sense that being a singer is somehow not respectable, and that perhaps his uncle feels he is not quite a gentleman. Being a professional singer seems to him not just disreputable, but also demeaning, unmanly – 'he set himself bitterly against the notion of being dressed up to sing before all those fine people who would not care about him except as a wonderful toy'.

So Daniel is the natural, gifted singer who does not want to sing, and his opposite number is Mirah, a young Jewish woman who has sung, or been made to sing, since she was a child. Dragged around theatres by her father, she has performed against her will and shares Daniel's disgust at being used as a plaything – 'it was painful that he boasted of me, and set me to sing for show at any minute, as if I had been a musical box'. Mirah has a sense of alienation and dehumanisation, the feeling that people don't love her for herself, but only for as much as she entertains them. There is a hint that Mirah's father has attempted to prostitute her out to rich men. Singing, then, can be a slippery slope, down which one could slide away from respectable society into its dark, hidden depths. If singers are treated like objects, slaves even, they are deprived of autonomy and dignity, so being a singer can be a wretched, demeaning profession.

It is left to the musician Klesmer to make a stronger claim, and to stand up for the right of musicians to be regarded more highly than as mere entertainers: 'We are not ingenious puppets, sir; who live in a box and look out on the world only when it is gaping for amusement . . . We count ourselves on level benches with legislators.' If George Eliot is here deliberately echoing the line from Shelley's 'A Defence of Poetry' – 'Poets are the unacknowledged legislators of the world' – she is making a case for singing to be elevated to a higher status. This links back to something I said in the foreword, the idea that singing is 'good' for us, that it is morally uplifting, and it's an idea that recurs in poems and novels. In Longfellow's poem, 'The Singers', the job of the singer is to awaken spirituality and godliness in the hearts of those hearing the song: 'God sent his Singers upon earth/With songs of sadness and of mirth/That they might touch the hearts of men/And bring them back to heaven again.' There's a holy, transcendent role to singing; as opposed to singing as entertainment, which can be corrupting and lowering, it's an explicitly religious interpretation, aligning singers with priests and preachers, charged with saving the souls of their fellow men. A heavy responsibility, you might think.

Even ordinary people can tap into this spiritual uplift

when they sing. There is a description in John Cheever's *The Wapshot Scandal* of a group of carol singers, who look ordinary and mundane in their outdoor clothes, 'but the moment they began to sing they were transformed . . . The carolers seemed absolved and purified as long as the music lasted, but when the final note was broken off they were just as suddenly themselves.' The effect of singing may be short-lived, only lasting as long as the song, but it is transformative and redemptive, and morally uplifting. In *Daniel Deronda*, Klesmer voices a similar view: that in order to save singers from the ambiguity of their position, from being regarded as tramps on the stage, performing monkeys, anyone's plaything, they had to be lifted up and sanctified.

This is idealisation, pure and simple, and singers are uniquely vulnerable to it. More than actors, they are seen to be 'themselves' in performance; what they offer is a direct expression of their own inner self, or soul, not the portrayal of a character (even though they may in fact be doing exactly that, singing lyrics written by others, or singing the tale of a character not themselves, or singing *in* character). The audience will tend to assume that the 'I' speaking (singing) is the person they see before them. And as such, their responses to the music, their projections and imaginings, become fused with what they imagine to be the personality of the singer. When reading reviews of *Bedsit Disco Queen*, I couldn't help noticing how often my writing voice was compared to my singing voice. The comments were positive, and lovely, my 'voice' being described as warm or approachable; down to earth and likeable. But making the link between the two voices was interesting to me, suggesting that many listeners already liked 'me', or felt that they did, because they liked my singing voice, and readily identified my writing voice as belonging to the same person.

In the 2009 novel *The Song Is You* by Arthur Phillips, a young singer called Cait apparently enjoys the attentions of an obsessive fan, but towards the end of the book she encounters a different character, Stan, who seems to like her not only for her voice but for herself: her voice is 'not the most interesting part of you, by a mile'. She ends up dating Stan, who says to her, 'If your job was dressing up as a rabbit in a theme park, would you want me to come visit you and pretend you were a real rabbit?' In other words, singing is a form of pretending. It is not who you really are. Anyone who forms a relationship with The Singer, in which they require her to act at all times like The Singer, is asking her to carry the make-believe elements of her job into her real life.

As a lyric writer, I am aware that songs written in the first person have more power, and an audience will connect more readily with them. But I am also aware that it will be taken for granted that every 'I' I sing represents the real me. Writing a song called 'Oh, The Divorces!' might have been asking for trouble (many listeners assumed I had recently divorced), and following it up with a track about visiting a singles bar in which I sang 'I pull off my ring as I push my way in/Won't be needing it here' seemed to confirm that, yes, 'I' really *had* ended my marriage and was now out on the dating scene. I'm regarded as a confessional songwriter, but one way in which it is possible to maintain a sense of privacy, or some mystery about the meanings of songs, is to blur the moments when 'I' really means me, and when it means someone else entirely.

Some singers and writers are understood to write 'in character' – Elvis Costello, for instance, or Randy Newman – because the characters they create are so obviously not themselves, and are either highly exaggerated or satirical creations or, in the case of Randy Newman, a monstrous opposite, who could not be mistaken for Randy himself. I don't do anything as extreme as that, so the assumption that 'I' means 'I' is easier to make, but it can be frustrating, and is another way in which the skill or decision-making involved in writing and singing can be overlooked in favour of a romantic belief that the artist is always engaged in the pursuit of self-expression. This simply isn't the case. Something is being expressed, yes, and it may be something heartfelt and true, but it may not be about *myself* or my own feelings.

So when we respond to a singer, often we don't really see or hear the actual person; we see and hear an imagined version of them, a projection of our own needs and desires. As Virginia Woolf wrote in *Jacob's Room*, 'Nobody sees any one as he is, let alone an elderly lady sitting opposite a strange young man in a railway carriage. They see a whole – they see all sorts of things – they see themselves . . . ' When we hear a singer, much of the experience is actually happening inside our own heads, and is a mixture of memory, desire, expectation and need – we hear what we expect to hear, or what we want and need to hear. If listeners tend to idealise singers, then the love an audience has for your voice can sometimes feel threatening to the singer as a person. It can make singers anxious that perhaps listeners want *too* much, more than the singer is willing or able to give. The biographies of troubled artists offer examples that bear this out, and when I talk to other singers there can be a recognition of this kind of feeling, but it isn't often understood or mentioned by people who write about music, especially if they are writing from the position of fan. It takes an imaginative leap for a writer who loves singing or a particular singer to move beyond their own pleasures as the listener and get inside the head of the singer. This is where fiction can bridge the gap, offering a way into that understanding, and it's why I want to look at certain novels which say things I haven't seen written down elsewhere. Only recently I discovered the novel *Bel Canto* by Ann Patchett, published in 2001, and it has stayed in my mind as a book that places a singer at the centre of its plot and in which I recognised and identified with much of what happens. Most of what we read about singers is journalism, which can be accurate and insightful but at its worst can simply repeat cliches that ultimately prevent us from getting to the truth of the matter. Those in the know – the singers themselves – might have other stories to tell, but someone needs to ask the right questions in order to access those stories. A novel can go further, inviting us to inhabit characters who take us beyond our own experiences. *Bel Canto* does this very well, dramatising the effect singers can have on those around them and the obsessive feelings that can be evoked. It is set in an unnamed Latin American country, where one night a glittering party full of international guests at the Vice

President's residence is stormed by a group of terrorists who take everyone hostage, including the party's star guest, an American operatic diva called Roxane Coss.

Glamorous and starry, she is an otherworldly being in their midst, bathed in an unearthly glow, and their reactions to her are all overreactions, or coloured by their own imaginations: 'No one could see her objectively anyway. Even those who saw her for the first time, before she had opened her mouth to sing, found her radiant, as if her talent could not be contained in her voice and so poured like light through her skin.' Before the terror attack takes place she performs to the crowd and has a spiritual, in fact explicitly religious impact on them: 'Her voice was so pure, so light, that it opened up the ceiling and carried their petitions directly to God . . . '

During the long siege that follows the hostage-taking, one of the guests, Mr Hosokawa, becomes more and more obsessed with her. It is not the reality of her that he desires, but an idealised version, and he doesn't really like to think of her as a body: 'It made him uncomfortable to notice the supreme athleticism of her mouth, to see so clearly her damp pink tongue when she opened up wide and wider still.' This is a dangerous kind of love: the kind of love that no one can live up to, that can only end in disappointment, and even turn to hate.

There is a young priest among the hostages, who also falls under her spell. He has long been an opera fan but feels guilt for the pleasure he gets; the singing fills him with a kind of longing, which is akin to desire. So he consoles himself by coming up with the idea that it is really a kind of religious rapture that she inspires. Yet there is a paradox – listening to Roxane sing, he thinks, 'God's own voice poured from her', and yet just a couple of lines later, 'It was as if the voice came from the center part of the earth' Well, which is it? Is the voice God's voice, from heaven above, or something elemental, earthy? There is a tension between the disembodied spirit quality of the voice, and the fact that it can only exist, can only be expressed at all, via the medium of a human body, with all the earthly connotations that brings. The ideal or the reality, which is it that the listener prefers?

Ann Patchett makes it clear that Roxane Coss is in every sense a flawed, mortal creature, and as we learn more about her, so the contrast between her humanity and the saintly version of her created by her listeners becomes ever more obvious. She is aware, for instance, of the power her voice gives her over others, and is not above exploiting this power. She is also proudly aware of her status, and takes comfort from this during their predicament: 'Maybe there would be a bad outcome for some of the others, but no one was going to shoot a soprano.'

Throughout the book, though others project onto her their need for her to represent something pure, aspirational, heavenly, her behaviour reveals her to be quite worldly, even venal. Her reason for being there in the first place is purely financial: 'I thought about declining. I declined several times until they came up with more money.'

And the moment which is most at odds with her admirers' image of her comes when she realises that the dire situation they are in may actually work out well for her in the end, as the story of the hostage-taking will increase her fame and so her value: "'So if I get out of here alive I can double my price?'" Surrounded by people who are, in various ways, going a bit mad over her singing, she can coldly calculate the effect this is all having on her future fees. It reminds us that as well as being a vocation, and offering something transcendental to the listener, singing is also a job, it is how some of us pay the bills. And this makes singers more prosaic about singing and what it means, sometimes weary of other people's attempts to elevate what they do.

Even Roxane's speaking voice exerts power over people. She talks on the phone to the priest's friend, another music lover, and in a moment of gushing fan behaviour, he asks her just to say the names of some operas down the phone to him:

'"*La Bohème*," she said. "*Così fan tutti*."

"Dear God," Manuel whispered . . . He was paralyzed by her voice, the music of speaking . . . '

This is funny, in its extremity. The ludicrous, over-the-top reaction of the fan to the object of their worship can't help but seem silly. No one can bear the weight of all this implied significance and the reactions to Roxane become meaningless, fabrications of the imagination. It's a novel that is very astute about the way in which 'fans' can become delusional, and the disillusionment that would surely result if they could get inside their idol's head.

None of this is to say that singers don't want or need to be loved – they do, of course – but there is tension in the gap between being loved for yourself and being loved for something that is not real. And an audience's tendency to idealise can make a singer believe that in order to be loved, the singing has to be perfect, or aspire to perfection; that faults will be judged and the self disliked for them, when of course the opposite can be true. Wayne Koestenbaum explains in his book how he loves Maria Callas above all because she made mistakes and 'seemed to value expressivity over loveliness'. I would count Björk as that kind of singer. I remember a television programme in which someone said that, in contrast to many classical singers who strive only to use the most beautiful part of the voice, the 'filet', Björk was prepared to use 'the whole animal'. Similarly, Koestenbaum describes Callas's voice as 'a set of sounds on the verge of chaos – but enjoyably so'.

Around Callas there grew up an enormous cult of personality and a strong bond between what people saw as the calamities of her personal life and the faults of her singing. Loving her, they could sympathise with both – 'we loved the mistakes because they seemed autobiographical', writes Koestenbaum. The audience were drawn in and involved, they felt they had a part to play in the construction of her singing performances; the sympathetic listener was needed in order to complete the singing: 'if her notes had a tendency to wobble, to grow harsh, then this possibility of failure gave her fans a function. The infallible performance does not require an audience.' Koestenbaum points out a particular moment in a rendition of an aria where she holds 'an awkward high note for its full value, even though the tone is unpleasant; she outstares the ugliness ... During the harsh high note, we are closer to Callas. We befriend her.'

She reveals her vulnerability, her humanity at these moments, and we want this from singers more than we want their technical perfection.

But oh, how hard it is for singers to believe this, and to feel it to be true.

4

SINGING INTO A VOID

Who is your favourite singer? It's a question I'm often asked, not surprisingly, and my answer is usually the same: Dusty Springfield.

I was born in 1962, and Dusty's career hit its peak around 1964, so as a singer she must have always been there, soundtracking my life. Yet no one in my house had any of her records. The radio must often have been playing her big 1960s hits, but I certainly wasn't hearing them at home. The songs seeped into my consciousness so that when I began to listen to her properly later on, I found I knew many of them by heart – but were they actually *her* versions I knew, or other people's? 'I Only Want to Be with You' I guiltily thought of as a Bay City Rollers song. 'How Can I Be Sure?' was by David Cassidy. 'You Don't Have to Say You Love Me' was Elvis Presley or even, God forbid, Guys 'n' Dolls. She was often on TV when I was a child, and I must have seen her, but again, the image that comes most readily to mind is a second-hand one, of someone impersonating her. She'd become famous for the flamboyant hand gestures she made while singing, and the joke was that she looked like she was directing the traffic. So while I have no true memory of seeing her performing, what I do remember is a comedy show, someone doing traffic policeman arms, and knowing that they were 'being' Dusty. I don't think it was meant unkindly, but still, there it was – she was famous enough to be the subject of a comedy impression, yet all I remember is the impression, not her.

However, I do know the first time I *heard* her. Elvis Costello was presenting a radio show, playing a selection of his favourite records, and as was usually the case with anything like that on the radio, I was taping it onto cassette. This was 1980, or maybe 1981. He had already introduced us to another of her signature tunes, 'I Just Don't Know What to Do with Myself', when he performed it on the *Live Stiffs Live* album in 1978, and that had been a revelation, opening my eyes to the possibility of liking Bacharach and David as well as punk; a difficult but heady idea, and one I would have to come back to later. Now on this radio show he played 'I Don't Want to Hear it Any More' from *Dusty in Memphis*, and for the first time I truly heard that voice – that smoky, husky, breathy, vulnerable, bruised, resigned, deliberate, sensual voice.

Ugh, all the same old words, and they won't do, will they? They won't do. Roland Barthes in his 1972 essay 'The Grain of the Voice' touched on this basic problem of music criticism, remarking snidely that 'the work (or its performance) is invariably translated into the poorest lin-guistic category: the adjective.' Well, it's hard to know what other part of the language to reach for when we want to describe something. If a voice is a noun, then we need an adjective to describe it, but they are of course limited and so we all reach for the same ones, and they wear thin from overuse. But where to find better ones, truer ones? If you'd never heard her voice, what words could summon it up in your imagination?

In her biography *Dusty*, Lucy O'Brien quotes Jerry Wexler, who produced *Dusty in Memphis* along with Arif Mardin, talking about the uniqueness of her sound: 'There were no traces of black in her singing, she's not mimetic . . . She has a pure silvery stream'. Silvery, I like that. I've always thought if Dusty's voice was a colour, it was silver. There is so much air in every note, and although the sound is rich, it has none of the chocolatey-brown of, say, Karen Carpenter's. It seems to exist higher up, almost suspended above our heads, literally transcendent. You look *up* to Dusty's voice, in every sense.

Neil Tennant pointed to the emotional tension in her singing, saying there's 'an intensity and desperation to her voice that's fantastically sensual'. Desperation: that's very observant. It's easy enough to hear the sensuality, of course, but to spot the undercurrent that makes her pierce you as much as soothe and seduce you, that's getting more to the heart of her. Of course, although she could be melodra-matic, particularly on the mid-1960s pop recordings, she was never a belter, and she was a singer who made use of the microphone. When she did project, there would be a fragility to it, and a feeling that she was covering it up with an element of bravado. There was a possibility that the voice might fail her, a note might break, although it never did. The slight huskiness is often commented on, the sound of being on the edge of laryngitis, which she suffered from recurrently. Some recording sessions were interrupted by her battling with throat problems – there are even songs where she sounds a little *too* close to actual voice loss, for example, 'Let Me in Your Way' from the album *A Brand New Me*.

But here's the terrible thing; the terrible, true thing that she thought, that maybe lots of singers think, which runs counter to all that we imagine it must feel like to be in possession of a unique and gorgeous voice that people love. This is what she once said: 'All I know is that I have a distinctive voice I don't particularly like listening to'.

Dusty Springfield is many people's favourite singer; she's not a challenging, left-field choice in any sense, and yet she also exemplifies the tortured artist, riddled with self-doubt, unsure of her worth and even her identity. Lucy O'Brien brilliantly chronicles how, as a slightly frumpy teenage ex-convent girl, Mary O'Brien took the irreversible decision, long before Madonna had apparently patented the concept, to reinvent herself, taking a gamble with her future and her sense of self, the consequences of which she couldn't possibly have anticipated. It must have seemed like an act of defiant self-liberation when she turned her back on the girl she'd been born as, and emerged with a new look – peroxide blonde hair glued into a beehive do, eyes almost lost under layers of thick black eyeliner and mascara – and a new name: Dusty Springfield. The look was all artifice: the sculptural creation that is a beehive hairdo was possibly the most unnatural style ever invented; the make-up deliberately over-the-top, too much. It was not about looking pretty, it was about looking different, both from everyone else and from her former self. And in this very difference there was an attempt to stand out, to seek attention, but in the same moment, to deflect that attention away from herself onto this new creation, this new fake persona, who could be everything Mary feared she couldn't be. Mary O'Brien could not be obliterated, she was still in there somewhere, hidden. As the early years of Dusty's career went by, and she became more successful, she exaggerated the look more and more – 'the bigger the hair, the blacker the eyes, the more you can hide' she is quoted as saying – and then found herself having to reconstruct her creation every single morning before she could face the world. No one was allowed to see her without the famous make-up or hairdo, and the sheer physical effort involved in all of it was exhausting and demoralising. What started out as a safety net became a trap. What she hadn't foreseen, and what looks so obvious in hindsight, is that in the act of creating a fake self she had dramatised and given physical expression to the very self-doubt which usually remains internalised. If artists often question their authenticity – and God knows they do – then what she had done in creating a fictional identity with which to confront the world made it absolutely sure that she would never be able to answer that question satisfactorily. She has talked about how intimidated she was during the sessions for *Dusty in Memphis* for

Atlantic Records, by the fact that those around her had worked with, and often talked about, Aretha. She had a tendency to think that the black session singers doing the backing vocals were 'the real thing' and she was a pop fake. And here's where I empathise completely with Dusty, having experienced the exact same doubts during the recording of EBTG's album *The Language of Life* in the US, coincidentally also for Atlantic Records, where I was singing with musicians who had worked with Michael Jackson and Whitney Houston. Understanding where and how you fit, and justifying your right to sing in the company of those who may be your singing superiors, is not always easy to sustain, and requires a degree of rationality and detachment which not many of us possess. It's a banal and repetitive tragedy that the pleasure a singer can provide does not reflect back to the singer her/himself, but instead hits a brick wall of self-doubt and discomfort.

In the recording studio Dusty's doubts were all about her voice. She would be demanding and perfectionist, both admirable qualities, essential for the making of good music, but when it came to the moment of recording the vocals she would turn those thoughts on herself like knives. She would have the volume in her headphones turned up as loud as possible, to the point where it was almost painful, and the effect would be overwhelming. That way she could let herself go into the experience, disappear inside a wall of sound, and so, just as she hid her physical appearance behind the mask of hair and make-up, she would hide even her voice. Jerry Wexler describes her doing this during the sessions for *Dusty in Memphis*, and is quoted in Lucy

O'Brien's biography saying that he always encouraged singers to have the sound fairly quiet in their headphones so they would project more, but Dusty had insisted on setting it at ear-splitting volume. 'There was no way she could hear herself – it was like she was singing into a void.'

If you're singing into a void, casting your voice out there into a black hole, the implication is that you want your voice to go away, to disappear. Some of the pleasure of singing is purely physical, an athletic enjoyment of using the body, stretching muscles, working up a sweat. You don't have to hear yourself in order to do this, and if you're unsure about the quality of what you hear then the enjoyment may be greater if you *can't* hear yourself. Singing in a choir, your voice can vanish among all the others, you are part of one big communal sound and no one is listening to you in particular. But as a solo singer, especially a famous and loved solo singer, this luxury is usually denied. You must be heard, and you must hear yourself. Dusty tried to escape hearing herself as a way of escaping confrontation with that which disappointed her, but I wonder also whether she suffered from that confusion between her voice and her person, whether she perceived doubts about her voice as in fact doubts about her value as a person, even about her existence as a real, authentic person. Was she trying to make 'Dusty' disappear, and be Mary O'Brien when she sang? Or did she want to be neither: was she trying to disappear altogether, to become no one, just a voice, not even a voice she wanted to hear, just the sound coming out of her, going nowhere?

As her career moved on, and she left behind the glory of

the British pop hits and the magnificence of albums like *Dusty in Memphis*, she really did begin to get lost, wandering a path with no obvious musical or career signposts to follow. She had matured as an artist, and at the very point when she should have been reaching a pinnacle in terms of success, her audience began to dwindle. *Dusty in Memphis*, released in 1969 and one of the greatest albums ever made, sold relatively poorly and was fairly soon deleted. *Cameo*, released in 1973, was a complete flop. It's one of my favourite records. I sing along with it and wish I had her voice. I fantasise that this is my new album, that all those musicians and backing singers are there for me, and that I am the voice at the centre of it all. I don't have Dusty's range, and I wish I did. If I could sing those songs the way she sang them, I'd be so proud, is what I think. I'd be fulfilled. I know it isn't true; I know it isn't as simple as that, and yet I fall into the same trap as every deluded listener. It's what singing does to us. It makes us so happy that we imagine it must come from happiness, mustn't it? Otherwise, it just doesn't seem fair. That we should be having all the fun.

5

NO SINGING

> I make up new notes, ones that don't belong
> anywhere near the chords I'm playing, and I sing
> those. People must think, *It's so nice of them to let
> that deaf girl sing.*
>
> Kristin Hersh, *Paradoxical Undressing*

It was punk that gave birth to the idea of the non-singer.
Rock music may have been full of unconventional vocalists before this – from Dylan through to Tom Waits and Lou
Reed – but they at least bore traces of previous singers and
singing styles, whether it was the nasal twang of country, the
semi-speaking of traditional folk delivery, or the small-
hours, cigarette-y jazz drawl. And, of course, rock albums
have long credited the singing to a 'vocalist', or told us who
is on 'lead vocals' rather than mentioning the word singing.
It's debatable whether this is a form of pretension – it's *more*

than singing – or deprecation – it's not *really* singing – but perhaps it's both, in the sense that rock's approach to singing sought, from the very start, to be both more and other. And from the 1950s onwards, parents accidentally watching rock and roll and then pop groups on TV would all declare in unison, 'They can't sing!' and 'You can't hear the words!', pointing out, as though their kids hadn't noticed – and as though it wasn't *the whole point* – the yawning gulf that separated these vocalists from the ones who'd gone before, the crooners, the tuneful serenaders, the sellers of songs.

Punk opened the door to a whole new attitude towards singing, the concept of deliberately not-singing, or not singing properly. Making a vocal sound that could not be described as even *trying* to sing in a way that would have been recognised as such by previous generations. And not because this era was bereft of talent and spawned a generation of singers sharing a unique inability to hold a tune, but because the performers were making choices that were intended to challenge the very idea of what singing was supposed to be.

Listening to Johnny Rotten, you couldn't possibly believe in his delivery as a 'natural' way of singing. It's completely improbable to picture an early rehearsal, at which the band started up the opening riff of, say, 'Pretty Vacant' and Johnny just opened up his mouth and that was the sound that came out. No, you could be sure that a lot of thought had gone into that sound; that it was a style of singing that embodied a whole attitude towards singing and music. Inspired no doubt by his immediate forebears the New York Dolls and Iggy Pop, Johnny Rotten's voice nonetheless had none of their more traditional raw masculinity, and in eschewing that apparently central tenet of rock singing he gave birth to something new: a sound that was fairly gender-neutral, expressive without being melodramatically emotional, and rebellious without buying into the rock notion that rebelliousness was inherently masculine. He sounded whiny, more oppressed than all-powerful, and slightly desperate. Every note he sang had 'I KNOW I CAN'T SING' stamped all over it, and it opened the floodgates for a generation of boys and girls to experiment and have fun while breaking all the rules about what singing should sound like.

I think of Poly Styrene as an example of someone who would probably never have got near a microphone in any other generation – almost the epitome of the non-singer, she could barely carry a tune, had no vibrato, nothing much to speak of in the way of range, and I absolutely loved her. Sheer force of will and strength of personality meant that she shone on stage, like a creature born to be there, delivering songs about modern society and its oppressive power over the individual with an irrepressible sense of joy. Simon Frith, in *Performing Rites*, says that her voice was the antithesis of femininity – 'it is not sweet or controlled or restrained' – and that this was a very conscious move on her part: 'its "unmusicality" is crafted. It is necessary for the song's generic impact.' In other words, she isn't just accidentally singing 'badly', there's a point being made. She seemed the embodiment of a free spirit, and as such was inspirational to timid little teenage me. If rules about what constituted 'good singing' were rigidly enforced, we would never have heard her, and the world would be a poorer place.

And what about Mark E. Smith? Can Mark E. Smith 'sing', in any conventional sense of the word? You'd have to say no, of course not, but in every other sense he can deliver a vocal like no one else, and in single-handedly inventing a vocal tic – an extra syllable at the end of every line, half grunt, half exasperated outburst: 'AH!' – that defines and identifies him, he too carved out a singular place for himself in the story of singing.

After a while, the danger was that new-wave non-singing developed its own set of cliches, which hardened and set and became vocal conventions in their own right. Foremost among these was the punk 'yelp'. A musicologist would have to pinpoint where we heard it first, and I'm not the person to do that, but Patti Smith was certainly doing it on *Horses* – listen to 'Gloria', for instance, where on these lines, 'look out the window see a sweet young thing' and 'oh she looks so fine', she ends each phrase by concluding with an upward, swooping yelp. Who else? Siouxsie Sioux, obviously, more noticeably on the early tracks like 'Love in a Void' and 'Metal Postcard'; and if there was a tape of it, which thankfully there isn't, you'd hear me doing it on my infamous version of 'Rebel Rebel' from what we might call The Wardrobe Sessions, my first attempt at singing during a rehearsal with my first band, Stern Bops. Pretty soon it had become an obvious cliche, a shorthand way of doing punky singing, and the yelpiness transmuted into a rather arch tone of voice. And when even that seemed too melodramatic, a post-punk style of absolutely deadpan non-singing became more prevalent from groups like Scritti Politti, Gang of Four and The Raincoats.

What this all adds up to is the fact that, just as punk allowed you to learn three chords and form a band, equally it enabled you to take hold of the microphone, position yourself at the front of the stage, and call yourself the Lead Singer, even if you couldn't sing. And this could be liberating even for those who pre-dated the movement, a good example being Marianne Faithfull, whose 1979 *Broken English* album is a masterpiece of punk-inspired reinvention. Alexis Petridis reviewed its 2013 reissue and accurately described the sea change in her singing which the album displayed: 'In the 60s, her voice was prim and weirdly stilted . . . Damaged by the excesses of the preceding years, her husking vocals on *Broken English* seemed not merely ravaged, but imperious and defiant . . . She sounded like she was telling someone to go and fuck themselves even when she wasn't.'

The changed sound of Faithfull's voice may have been a result of physical damage wrought by years of a lifestyle that did little to protect it. But that change in attitude, that defiant stance of singing every line like you're telling someone to go and fuck themselves – that, I think, was inspired by punk; the way that punk's rebellious style moved on from the old macho exclusively rock and roll cliches made it particularly liberating for female singers.

Paradoxical Undressing, the Kristin Hersh book from which this chapter's opening quote is taken, is brutally honest about Hersh's own singing and her approach to performing. Her band Throwing Muses got started in the 1980s and were part of the indie scene that in many ways was really America's punk rock moment. Kristin's thoughts about singing place her firmly in the punk-inspired camp of non-singers, and having spotted her on Twitter, I made contact and asked if she'd answer a couple of questions. I told her how much I loved that line from her book, which is so self-deprecating and funny, and asked her if she felt part of a punk generation, inspired by the flowering of a style of non-singing:

KRISTIN: I have one rule in the studio: 'no singing', meaning 'no faking'. Which probably pertains to guitar parts as well: no chops, no imitating, no telling the song what to do. A real vocal is a textural expression. Maybe the kind you croon to your baby, maybe the kind you yell when you drop something on your foot, but it must be determined by the song or it will never resonate with the listener. And if it's embarrassing? So much the better!

ME: I also love the bits in your book which are your conversations with Betty Hutton, where she stresses the importance of entertaining people, putting on a per-formance, and you are quite resistant to this. Do you still feel that is true to your ideas about singing and per-forming or have you come round to her point of view at all?

KRISTIN: I know that people who 'perform' out-perform me by music business standards, but I don't think they're musicians. Rather, they're *performers*. My job is to disappear inside a song, to shake off the outside rather than show it off. I can be practically drooling on stage, with my eyes rolling back in my head, but at least the song is on stage instead of me. It's *never* pretty, though.

ME: What is your relationship with your voice? Do you love it? Does it feel like an intrinsic part of you or something separate? Do you worry about it, fear for it, take care of it like a baby? Or are you blasé and carefree about it?

KRISTIN: The most my voice is capable of is telling the truth. I like the truth (sometimes).

For Kristin, singing is about getting at some kind of truth, and if this comes at the risk of embarrassment, well, so be it. Punk was big on notions of authenticity and credibility, and so there's a somewhat theoretical mindset present in this take on singing. Sometimes I think that my own version of how to sing is more prosaic, akin to the advice Noel Coward gave to actors, namely, 'Speak clearly, don't bump into the furniture.' Applied to singing, I suppose this translates as, 'Know the words and try to sing in tune.' But how does it square with my admiration for all this non-singing? What if ideologically you bought into all these concepts, and felt a kinship with Siouxsie and Poly Styrene, and the not-even-trying-to-sing approach of people like The Raincoats and Delta 5, but then, when you started singing, you realised you had a voice which was, well, not like that?

When I sang for the very first time, from inside that wardrobe, I made a stab at impersonating the voice of the time, and it was all Siouxsie Sioux swoops and yelps. But after I emerged from the shadows, I never sang like that again. Realising that I *could* actually sing, it seemed like an act of the greatest inauthenticity to cover it up, to try to sing badly, to put on an alternative voice. And so I started to seek out others who really sang, who were part of the musical world I loved but who imported into it something of the music from outside.

A brief digression on hairstyles: the reason I had all those dark curls in my early 1981 Cherry Red publicity pics was because I had had my hair permed in a vain attempt to look like Lesley Woods, the guitar-toting feminist frontwoman of Birmingham band the Au Pairs. It didn't quite work because I went to the local hairdresser in my home village of Brookmans Park and he was an expert at the kind of perms requested by my mum and her contemporaries, so the result was a more neat, housewifey 'do' than the unruly black mop I'd been hoping for. It looked better as it grew out, and I had it permed several more times, each time believing that it would transform me at a stroke into my current heroine. If the music I was into had been all about proving that anyone could join a band and anyone could sing, then here was Lesley suggesting that, while that might be all very well up to a point, there was still no substitute for someone who actually could sing.

She was the exception that proved the rule. Someone who would and should have been a singer at any point in pop music history. Husky-voiced, sensual, with an almost unheard-of-for-the-times vibrato, she was the second singer after Patti Smith who truly inspired me. I saw the Au Pairs live several times in 1980, and when their first album, *Playing with a Different Sex*, came out in 1981 I fell for it heavily. Singing along with 'Headache for Michelle' and 'Repetition' revealed to me more about how I might sound, and I borrowed from her my tendency to end a note with a wavery tremolo of a breath, the first hint of something 'jazzy' in my singing. Of course, when required, she could do the mandatory shouty voice too, as on songs like 'Come Again' and 'Dear John', but even then she had a commanding presence that came from the confidence of knowing what she was doing.

And so Lesley Woods led me to Billie Holiday. Maybe I read a review that made the connection, or just heard some echo in her lazy phrasing, a hint of gravel in the tone. Whatever it was, it meant that I was soon listening to someone who really was a singer. True, Billie Holiday was no smooth-toned crooner, but still, it wasn't hard to hear the difference between her and Poly Styrene or Siouxsie Sioux. She herself might not have believed in her own legend (music journalist Ian Penman recently sent me an extraordinary snippet of her speaking, captured on a bootleg tape: 'I'm tellin' you – me and my old voice, it just go up a little bit and come down a little bit. It is not LEGIT. I do not got a legitimate voice'), but for me there was no doubting her. And it was partly because I was beginning to realise that I too could maybe sing 'properly' that I became more drawn to other singers who transcended the limits of post-punk non-singing. I bought a Billie Holiday album in a garish orange sleeve, one of many *Best Of* compilations and all my budget could stretch to, and discovered songs like 'I Cover the Waterfront' and 'My Man'. From the securely hip world of my punk and post-punk singles, I wandered sideways, off the beaten track and into jazz. Post-punk sort of allowed this, in that it was very welcoming to anything that wasn't rock, but still, the preference was for the more experimental end of jazz. Billie Holiday wasn't exactly that. She sang these songs straight, but with a rawness that allowed rock fans to relate to her. Downstairs, my mum and dad had their Ella Fitzgerald and Frank Sinatra, but I found it harder to admit to liking those. Billie Holiday they weren't so sure about, and that worked in her favour as far as I was concerned. I learned many of her songs, tried to imitate her vibrato, and by the time I met Ben, I was already wondering if there was a way to combine that kind of singing with the music I'd played up until then. If my singing began to sound more 'jazzy', well, that was down to Billie and her influence. But this new direction would raise a whole set of problems to do with questions of ease and difficulty, and the perceived profundity of different types of singing.

Academic and critic Aidan Day – who, coincidentally, was my first English tutor at Hull University – writes (as quoted in Simon Frith's *Performing Rites*) about Bob Dylan that he has a voice which 'at once solicits and rebuffs. The gratifications it offers are uncomfortable ones. It is a pattern of invitation and rejection in which the audience – alienated from easy absorption into the music and denied relaxation – is required to attend closely to the transactions between voice and words.' The implication is that a difficult voice forces you to listen more closely, make more effort, attend more minutely to what is being sung. You can't just swoon as you would into the arms of a sweeter, smoother voice: you have to pay attention, and this implies that you will take the singing more seriously and get something deeper out of it. And so, the non-singing style of punk and its aftermath meant that you could immediately impress upon an audience, and perhaps more to the point, upon music critics, the notion that you were serious, worthy of close scrutiny; that your work was demanding, and by implication, clever. If, in contrast, you had a voice which was *not* uncomfortable, which in fact had at its core a tone that could easily soothe and charm, then you could be accused of being shallow, banal, merely relaxing. Whether or not that is necessarily a bad thing is entirely a matter of opinion, but it has to be said that for a long time in the history of modern pop it seemed to be taken for granted by many journalists that there was something suspect about what might be termed 'proper' singing.

6

LEAD SISTER

Who embodies all that I've just said about a style of singing perceived to be smooth and relaxing more than Karen Carpenter? With her luxurious mink of a voice, all softness and warmth, no sharp edges in sight, she is regarded, for good or bad, as the epitome of the soothing singer – yet you don't have to dig very deep into her story to see how jarring, how incomplete and careless that description is. I've occasionally been compared to her, and while I take that as nothing but a compliment, I'm also aware of darker similarities between us: problems and inconsistencies around singing that exist (or existed) in sharp contrast to all the surface ease. I've said before that I used to think of myself not so much as 'a singer', as 'someone who sings', and delving into Karen's biography it's clear that at the start of her career, and possibly even well into it, she regarded herself as The Carpenters' drummer, who

happened to sing. In the early days she sang from her position behind the drums, which I've always considered one
of the coolest of musical accomplishments, but this wasn't
allowed to last. It's obvious to us now, but it was a surprise
to her at the time, that when people heard her sing they
were overwhelmed. Richard's piano playing may have been
fine, her drumming perfectly good, but her *voice*, well, that
was something different. And so of course audiences, man-
agers, record companies, they wanted to hear her sing
more, and they wanted to see her sing.

Dragged out from behind the kit and made to stand
centre stage, it was immediately apparent that she lacked the
stage presence to do so, and wasn't a natural performer.
Those around her felt that the drum kit was a security blanket, something she hid behind, and so they did her the great
kindness of taking that security blanket away and throwing
it in the bin. In Randy L. Schmidt's biography *Little Girl
Blue*, she is quoted as saying, 'It hurt me that I had to get up
and be up front. I didn't want to give up my playing.
Singing was an accident. Singing seriously came long after
the drums.' Interpreted as weakness, maybe her love of playing drums was really an act of self-knowledge, an
understanding of what was good for her and where her
limits, or her desires, lay. 'Lead Sister' she had printed on her
T-shirt, which might seem self-deprecating – oh, I'm
nobody really, just Richard's sister – but might also have
been a statement of intent: you call me the lead singer but
it's not how I see myself. I'm a team player, part of a group,
a family; I can't quite take this image of myself seriously.

Schmidt recounts how Terry Ellis of Chrysalis Records,

whom she became close to for a while, came to see The Carpenters play live in 1975 and was shocked by how unprofessional Karen was on stage, how little stage presence she seemed to have: 'She hadn't the slightest idea how to use a stage. She did everything wrong ... She'd sing a song, and when the guitar player or drummer played a little solo she'd turn her back on the audience and sort of click her fingers and had no interrelation with the audience ...'

In other words, she behaved like a muso on stage, like a jazz performer, like someone more wrapped up in the music than in showing off to the crowd. In a different context this would have been tolerated, respected even. Maybe she was cut out for an entirely different kind of musical career – one where she could have sung from her drum kit, clicked her fingers during the guitar solos, closed her eyes and lost herself, let the audience go hang. But this was light entertainment she was caught up in. Big-time showbiz. And it had rules. She hadn't known what those rules were, and had never signed up to them, but as time went by, she was reminded more and more that she needed to learn them, and needed to modify her behaviour. She learned that 'she did everything wrong'. She was taught how to move about the stage, how to reach down and touch the outstretched hands of the front row, how to really *be* the focus of attention.

At one point, in an attempt to rectify the attention imbalance between the two of them – to enable Richard to be a bit more the star – they rigged up a mirror above his piano and angled it so that the audience could clearly see his hands flying up and down the keyboard. If they could *see* what

Richard was doing, the thinking apparently went, they'd come to their senses, realise that he was the true talent of the band. Karen herself seems to have partly agreed with this, sharing in the sense that her brother was unfairly disregarded, and that it was by mere accident that the audience loved her. 'Because I'm the lead singer I get all the credit,' she said. 'They think I did it, and all I do is sing. He's the one that does all the work.'

I agree with her that focus on the singer can be unbalanced, but, as I wrote in an earlier chapter, it reflects a general truth about audiences – that there is only so much of the instrumental music they can understand and appreciate. Much of the detail and subtlety of a musical arrangement can pass listeners by, as they simply don't have the technical expertise or knowledge to recognise how much skill may be involved, or what level of talent they are witnessing. But singing is different; audiences believe and feel that they can understand singing, and latch onto the singer with gratitude – *this* we understand, *this* speaks to us. In the case of The Carpenters, most of us would agree that the audience was right: Karen was so clearly the best thing about the group. The songs are often great, yes, but the arrangements, the settings, the instrumentation, well, they don't always do her justice. Plus the softness, the sweetness – let's be honest, the schmaltziness – kept many of us at a distance for so long, and I can't be alone in sometimes wishing we could have heard Karen with someone else doing the music. So when she says 'all I do is sing. He's the one that does all the work', I also can't be the only one thinking, 'Honey, it was always all about your singing.'

It's never easy to define what it is that's great about a singer, but an observation made by Schmidt in his biography struck me as providing a clue. It's to do with the length of her phrases before she takes a breath. Listen to the opening of 'We've Only Just Begun', where she sings 'We've only just begun . . . to live' before she takes a breath. Many singers would pause and breathe after that 'begun', but she holds on and finishes the phrase before breaking.

And in 'Goodbye to Love', listen to where she sings 'Time and time again the chance for love has passed me by, and all I know of love is how to live without it'. Now, that's all in one breath. It's a convoluted, twisting piece of melody, so as you get further into the line and begin to be short of breath, it becomes harder to control the pitch of the voice. Try and do it yourself now; it's not easy. But listening to her, there is absolutely no indication of difficulty, it is the epitome of 'easy' singing: deceptive in that all the effort is engaged in the act of hiding the effort. In itself this might be a meaningless technical accomplishment, and not actually that challenging for any singer with reasonable breath control to do, but what's interesting to me is the fact that she *chose* to sing these long unbroken lines, almost the equivalent of a cinematic single long take – the passage I quoted from 'Goodbye to Love' reminds me of the three-and-a-half-minute tracking shot which begins Orson Welles's *Touch of Evil*. It's a style that has an entrancing effect on the listener: you are drawn in as she begins, and then find you are almost holding your breath, waiting for *her* to breathe, and it's a long time before she does, so you are held, suspended, hypnotised; just as in the cinema your eyes are glued to the screen, not wishing to interrupt the seamless flow. A pause in the delivery of a vocal while a breath is taken can sometimes release the tension, freeing the listener momentarily (though sometimes it's true that it can have the opposite effect – dramatic in-breaths can be used to heighten the sense of effort, to build anxiety in the listener), but in so many of her lines Karen takes few noticeable breaths, so you are held captive by the vocal performance, caught in her spell. It's very effective, and, along with the richness and warmth of her tone – so often commented on as to be almost taken for granted but still, unusually lovely, utterly and uniquely beautiful – it is, I believe, one of the sources of her power as a singer.

Also, you can hear how close she is to the mic; on 'We've Only Just Begun', at the end of the line 'white lace and promises', there is the very clear sound of her mouth opening. Nowadays you'd edit that out, cleaning up the gaps between lines of vocal, but it's an indication of how intimate she is with the mic. Many who worked with her noticed how much of a mic singer Karen was, how soft her voice was, how little projection she had. All this gave you the sense that you were really getting close to her, getting inside her thoughts, even; and the awful sadness of some of the songs – honestly, there is a Nico-like bleakness and air of futility to some of the Carpenters' lyrics – is at odds with the cheerfulness of the publicity photos, the flounciness of the dresses. She didn't write those lyrics, but she certainly sang them as if they came from the depths of her being.

I wouldn't presume to assign to her tragic early death a simplified reading of her problems with fame or performance; and people who know much more about anorexia than I do would surely point to the relevance of complex family relationships, and deep-rooted issues to do with self-worth and control. But it can't be wrong to at least acknowledge that for anyone struggling with such issues, the stage is probably not the safest place to be. And it's a reminder that talent – like beauty, or money – can't always save you, or counterbalance the forces that weigh you down.

So you might dream of having a voice like Karen Carpenter's, imagining it would make you happy, or at least fulfilled. At least you'd be sure of that one thing, wouldn't you? You'd be secure in your possession of a peerless talent, and that would be valuable, would count in your favour. The possession of something *extraordinary*, that's the goal. You could easily believe that having that singing voice would make the difference. And you'd be wrong.

7

YOU SOUND JUST LIKE YOU

I was in the loo at a nightclub once, years ago, when I was recognised as I washed my hands. It can't have been that long after 'Missing' was a hit as the request made of me was not for an autograph, or even a photo, but for me to sing a few lines of the song to prove that I was really *that* Tracey Thorn. And because I'd presumably had a few drinks – I must have done or I would have run a mile in the opposite direction – I agreed, and standing there at the sink I took a deep breath and sang, 'I step off the train, I'm walking down your street again, and past your door, but you don't live there any more.'

The girls stared and squealed at me, and grabbed each other, and the thing they said, which I took as the ultimate compliment, was: 'YOU SOUND JUST LIKE YOU!'

I knew what they meant, of course I did. That my voice really was my voice, the authentic sound that came out of my mouth, not some product of studio trickery and fakery. There's a naivety to this response, really, the idea that someone's voice can be manufactured for them in the studio – which is simply not as true as people think – and an old-fashioned regard for the virtues of vocal authenticity. But there's an important point to be made here, a timeless truth, which is that however much vocals can be manipulated, or fixed, or homogenised, finding your own voice – your unique, personal sound – is still the key ingredient in becoming a singer.

It's not even the case that your 'voice' is necessarily the raw sound you were born with; it may in fact be the 'voice' you choose to sing with, and which becomes your defining sound, the style by which you are identified. Richard Curtis once told me that during the making of the film *Notting Hill*, he visited the studio where Elvis Costello was recording 'She' for the closing credits. Costello apparently did several great run-throughs of the track, and then asked, 'Would you like me to do one as "Elvis Costello"?' Well, yes, of course they would, and what resulted was a performance of unadulterated, creepy, stalker-ish Costello menace, the last thing they needed for their purposes, but still, memorable to witness.

Similarly, when I worked with Green Gartside recently, recording a duet for my *Tinsel and Lights* album, he was a little nervous about his singing, and after a few attempts at the vocal, asked me, 'How Scritti do you want it?' By which he meant, I think, 'How much do you want me to sing it in that apparently artificial and sugary-sweetened tone of the classic Scritti Politti recordings?' But the truth

was, I had realised as soon as Green started to sing, that
there actually wasn't much artifice involved in the Scritti
vocal sound. He really did sound like that, from the
moment he opened his mouth. It was a great example of a
vocal style that may at some point have been 'created', but
has since become the 'natural' way in which that person
sings.

A significant part of 'finding your voice' is settling on what
accent to sing in. But if the accent you choose is not your
own, natural accent, have you actually found your voice, or
rather, invented your voice? For those of us from the UK
who sing pop or rock music the default setting is a US
accent, and yes, I am aware of how vague that sounds, and
that there are differences between the accents of Tennessee,
Brooklyn and the San Fernando Valley. But there's a
generic American accent that has long been accepted as a
natural and normal tone of voice for British singers to
adopt.

In the early rock and roll days, British singers copied the
American music they heard, which included singing in an
'American' accent – often an Afro-American accent, in
truth. They sang in the way they felt fitted the music, and
did their best to sing in what they thought was the correct
accent, but of course they were often wide of the mark,
having no real experience or understanding of the subtleties
of the accent they were copying. As a result, to American
ears they often still sounded very British – or at least, not
American. From the mid-1960s onwards British singers
moved away from this tendency as the idea of sounding

British took on its own validity, and then punk came along and said that it was corporate and fake to sing in a US accent, and introduced a whole slew of bands who used not just a British accent, but a very self-consciously working-class British accent, whether or not this was any closer to their speaking voices than an American accent would have been. It was a badge of honour, a mark of authenticity; singing 'in American' marked you out as a pop star, whereas the punk accent asserted your street credibility. There were some artists who ignored this, though; The Stranglers proved that they were not 'really punk' by adopting US accents, as did Elvis Costello, who in fact took it to extreme lengths. The first song I heard by him was '(The Angels Wanna Wear My) Red Shoes', and it seemed like a while since I'd heard anyone singing in such shameless American. I loved it immediately, and sang along with him at home, so perhaps it's no surprise that when I started singing with the Marine Girls, my accent was more American than was the norm within the indie scene at the time. My bandmates Gina and Alice both sang in markedly English accents, so there was an immediate discrepancy between the three of us. When we played at the Moonlight Club in London with Felt, Lawrence from the band came up to me afterwards and said I had 'sounded great, really American!' It was interesting to me that he considered this a compliment (although I shouldn't have been surprised, given that he himself was trying to sound like Lou Reed), but I understood, and I took it as such. It seemed that, despite punk and indie and the idea of being authentic and true to your roots, deep inside some of us still had the feeling that it just sounded *better* singing in a slightly American accent. When I met up with Ben at university in 1981, and we recorded our first EBTG single 'Night and Day', it felt obvious to sing a jazz standard in American. However, Ben still sang in the pastoral-influenced English accent of his early solo recordings, so on the B-side track, 'Feeling Dizzy', there are two competing accents. It's not that this doesn't work – and exactly the same clash would happen when I sang with Robert Wyatt on Working Week's 'Venceremos' – but still, it's intriguing to hear two singers, born within only a few miles of each other, adopting accents which originate thousands of miles apart.

Through the years, my accent would shift on occasion. After two years living in Hull and a few months of listening to Morrissey, I went a bit northern amid the American, so there is a line on *Eden*, during the song 'Even So', when in the midst of my usual accent I suddenly sing, 'It's joost that I fear you can't looove as you did before'. By the time of *Love Not Money*, and on into *Baby, the Stars Shine Bright*, I'd discovered country music and my American accent drifted further south, closer to the Mason–Dixon line, than ever before or since. I'd discovered how satisfying it is to accentuate the 'H' sound whenever it appears at the beginning of a word, particularly if that word is 'heaven', and on the songs 'Are You Trying to Be Funny?' and 'Heaven Help Me' I exploit it to the full, sounding more like Tammy Wynette than anyone born in Brookmans Park really has a right to. Over the next few albums my accent settles a bit, reverting to being more non-specifically US, until on *Walking Wounded* there are moments when I sing in a more British accent than ever before. 'Flipside' in particular, with its glottal stops and London vowels, is a different accent to any I had used before, and it continued on to *Temperamental*, on tracks like 'Hatfield 1980', 'Downhill Racer' and 'No Difference'. The influence was from Massive Attack, and the way they rapped in their own homegrown voices on tracks like 'Karma Coma', and it might even, I'm ashamed to say, have owed something to the mockney accents of Britpop. In the mid-1990s, sounding British went through something of a renewed vocal vogue. But I felt that I had finally come up with an accent that did feel properly mine – a hybrid, admittedly, the American slurring and softened consonants I'd always enjoyed now blended occasionally with harder British endings, closer to the sound of my natural speaking voice.

I think I've settled on this accent now, since I don't think twice about it when I sing. The solo albums I've made in recent years reveal no obvious changes. It seems to me that there are certain songs that require a subtle gradation of accent, and it's instinctive to blur the line between my real accent and the accent I've so often sung in. A little while ago I recorded some songs written by Molly Drake, singer-songwriter Nick Drake's mother. Her own versions are quintessentially English, her accent striking the now almost lost tones of Received Pronunciation, and this lends the songs an air of inaccessibility. They seem to belong so completely to another era, ensconced in the drawing room with all its politeness and reserve, that the dark emotions buried within them can go unheard. So I tried to sing them in a direct manner, as she does, while shaking off some of the more dated, middle-class features of the diction – and the obvious way to solve this was to subtly Americanise them, in order to gently tease out some of the blues-like inflections of her writing. It was a fine balance – trying not to lose what is distinctive and unique about them, while freeing them from some of the mannerisms that simply sound too artificial or old-fashioned for our tastes.

Recording a voice is a way of capturing it, and may even reveal to the singer something they didn't know was there. Wayne Koestenbaum writes of the singer Nellie Melba hearing her recorded voice for the first time and exclaiming, 'Heavens, it's *me*.' He adds that this aspect of revelation was one of the great claims of the early recording companies: 'The Victor Company promises, "A mirror may reflect your face and what is written there; but the Victrola will reflect and reveal your soul to you – and what is hidden deep within it."' You cannot hide from a recording of your voice, and what is revealed is far more than mere timbre, or range, or inflection. The implication is that the unique voice – whether we believe it to be entirely natural, 'authentic', or at least in part a created or discovered thing – opens up a direct conduit to the soul, or the personality.

Because of this we worry and fret about whether or not a singer's voice is 'mannered' or 'artificial', believing perhaps that this is a gross act of concealment or dishonesty, that in attempting to cover up one's natural voice, or add to it, or improve upon it, we are committing an act of subterfuge which is both sinister and untrustworthy. What are we trying to hide? Why are we trying to pass off mere fakery as the real thing?

Within pop there is a long tradition of the artificial, 'put-on' voice; indeed it's difficult to locate what we might call genuinely natural or 'real' voices, since there's almost always some element of pretence involved in the singing process. Nonetheless, some singers really do seem to have gone to the ends of the earth to dredge up a distinctive sound, and to have come back with a voice that can only be described as deliberately provocative. With these voices it's not even the case that they are imitating someone else, more that they are inventing something on the spot, for better or worse. Mick Jagger, for instance, is often accused of emulating black singers, but really, who? Who can you think of who actually sounded like that before Jagger 'imitated' them? It's a cartoon of a black singer, painted onto a balloon and then inflated, then put through a mangle, then through an amplifier. What comes out the other end is patently foolish and ridiculous, and turned him into one of rock's most admired singers, copied in his turn to this very day.

Simon Frith, in *Performing Rites*, says of the early days of rock and roll singing that it is salutary to note that white singers didn't just steal from black culture, 'they burlesqued it'. He quotes Bernard Gendron stating in *Rock and Roll Mythology: Race and Sex in Whole Lotta Shakin Going On*, that rock and roll introduced a lot of black artists to a white audience, but the audience then expected the performers to live up to their notions of authentically 'black' style, which they'd seen packaged and exaggerated by white singers. So people like Chuck Berry, Little Richard and Ray Charles, who all 'began their careers by singing the blues in a rather sedate manner ... later accelerated their singing speed, resorted to raspy-voiced shrieks and cries ... they went from singing less black (like Nat King Cole or the Mills Brothers) to singing more black' ... which was in turn borrowed back by more white performers, in a kind of escalation. We have become used to singing styles that were almost entirely artificial and mannered, and indeed regard them as the foundations of today's rock and pop music.

The 1970s was a good decade for unnatural voices, giving us, for instance, Elton John's incredibly elongated vowels and David Bowie's invented vowels. Bowie's voice always intrigues and delights me, not least for its unexpectedness. Listening to his hesitant speaking voice, and looking at that slight, fragile body, the beautiful clothes, the girlish bone structure, you'd imagine him having a singing voice as light as chiffon, a mere wisp of a thing. Then watch him take to the stage and bellow 'Jean Genie' at the audience and marvel at his vocal strength and power; it's a strongly masculine rock voice that comes from this supposedly ethereal being.

But these are voices that make no attempt to cover up their mannerisms, and their made-up nature is fully revealed when you try to sing along with them. How, after all, do you join in with Bryan Ferry doing 'Virginia Plain'? It's a glorious swooning concoction, but forces you to confront one of singing's great perils – the risk of ridicule. Dare to sing in this kind of voice and you throw caution to the wind; it could go either way. If people fall for it, and buy into it as being 'your' voice, you're home and dry, you've come up with something unique, which you own. But to get to that point takes courage, confirming the fact that in pop music, self-belief outweighs much else. I try to imagine the first Roxy Music rehearsal, where Bryan Ferry stalked up to the microphone and started singing, and I wonder if there were any startled looks, or if everyone in the room just decided to take him at his word and accept *that* as his singing voice.

In 1978, when Kate Bush released 'Wuthering Heights', I was too immersed in my punk records to like it. More than the fact that it featured piano – drippy – and referenced a novel – swotty – I struggled with the singing. That melo-dramatic, all-over-the-shop approach to vocal melody just screamed 'hippy' at me, and seemed to be the aural equiv-alent of shawls, beads, headdresses and candles, all of which I suspected Kate Bush was wearing or surrounded by while she recorded the vocal. It was this very flamboyance that imprinted itself on people's minds and made it so appealing to the amateur performer (still imprinted on my eardrums, eyeballs and indeed damaged psyche, is the memory of two friends' moving rendition at a Christmas karaoke party), but singing in that way, in *that* voice, steered the song close to the ridiculous. You could contend that the novel itself is somewhat manic and hysterical, so Kate Bush's vocal is true to the tone of her source material, and yet, what a gamble to take. It paid off, of course – four weeks at number one for a debut single about a Victorian novel isn't bad going – and proved once again that with rock and pop singing it's probably safe to say that you can never go too far in your quest to find a distinctive voice for yourself.

Listeners will follow you a long way if you keep them interested. The aim isn't necessarily to feel beholden to your innate voice, or to strive to produce a 'natural'-sounding voice, but above all to aim for one that has confidence in itself, and expresses something unique. That in itself is a form of naturalness, in that it's not about imitation – which you could regard as the ultimate artificiality – but striving for individuality, even if that means employing what might be regarded as 'mannerisms'. In the case of both Costello and Gartside, you could easily argue that they are mannered singers, with voices that have been artificially constructed; nevertheless, both have a strong sense that the 'voice' they have created is entirely their own. Would you like me to do one as 'Elvis Costello'? How Scritti do you want it?

8

A FIENDISH OBSTACLE RACE

It seemed likely that Green Gartside would have interesting things to say about singing. Renowned for being a great pop thinker and theorist, it was from his interviews in the *NME* in the late 1970s and early 1980s that I learned words like deconstruction and hegemony. I was still at school at the time, and not paying much attention to what was on offer there, so this was an education of sorts, albeit a patchy and piecemeal one. These interviews, though, and the songs that prompted them, were bracing and invigorating, like being dunked in the deep end of a pool of thought without any armbands on, or any real idea of how to swim. In an interview with the *Guardian*, Green himself admitted that during this period, 'the ratio of tactically deployed pop banality to smartarse references to Kant and Gramsci was occasionally uncomfortably high'. He gained a reputation for being exceptionally brainy, and for his unusual ability to offer a detached perspective on the music he was making; in other words, to deconstruct his own works and their meanings. Which is why it came as no surprise to me to hear him say, 'How Scritti do you want it?' Here was someone entirely aware of the competing elements of artifice and reality within the pop voice; someone who I suspected had given a lot of thought to the concept of singing, both his own and other people's.

So I was delighted when he agreed to talk to me about singing, and I thought it would be good to get started on simple terms. Steering clear of any attempt to impress him by asking about Roland Barthes (which I'm sure wouldn't have impressed him at all), I began with a nice obvious question:

ME: Did you always want to be a singer?

GREEN: Well, since childhood I always dreamed of being in a band. Punk made that a realisable aim. I didn't especially want to be the singer. That really fell to me by default.

ME: Yes, this is what happens to people, so much of it is an accident. There are the precocious kids who get up on tables at family weddings and sing to everyone, and who spend their lives in front of the mirror with the hairbrush microphone, but I suspect many of them never take it any further. So you end up with people like us at the front of the stage, the ones who got there by default. I often think I might have been happier at the back, maybe the bass player or something. I used to dream of being Gillian in New Order; I thought that really might have suited me better.

And what about inspiration? Did any singers inspire you? Do you even think inspiration is possible, or do we just borrow bits here and there, sound like people accidentally?

GREEN: Like you, perhaps I'm suspicious of romantic ideas of 'inspiration'. The voice is really all influences and anatomy. When I was a young boy my favourite singer was Paul McCartney. Other early favourites were Brian Wilson, Paul Rodgers from Free (I know!), Robert Wyatt, Robin Williamson, Martin Carthy, Captain Beefheart . . . lots, lots more . . . very varied. Favourites, but not clear influences. All white men (and Joni Mitchell) back then.

ME: And did you try to imitate them, on the way to finding your own voice?

GREEN: I'm sure I tried imitating them all on the way to 'creating' my own voice. I don't think my voice or anyone else's is 'natural' or 'unmediated' or 'unaffected'. To a greater or lesser extent I could and can sing in (or with?) voices other than that with which I'm associated. I think we probably all can.

ME: I think that's true up to a point, although I'd always be limited in terms of physical strength — I'd never be able to be a shouter, which I sometimes wish I could be.

But certainly, when I'm on my own and feeling unin-
hibited, I can 'put on' different voices and it's kind of
intriguing to imagine how different you might sound if
you used them. But I think once you've established yourself with one particular voice, you're not really allowed to
change it much. People would be freaked out, I think.

(I'm reminded at this moment of a piece I read on a music
blog, The Delete Bin, by a writer called Rob Jones, entitled
'8 Voices of Bob Dylan'. It's a fascinating piece, you can find
it online if you want to read it all, but he starts out by saying
that when people object to Bob Dylan by stating that they
don't like his voice, 'my reaction in recent years is to wonder
which voice they happen to be talking about. After all, Bob's
used more than one.' And then he goes on to provide a clear
and distinct description of them all, from the early Guthrie-
isms of 'The Young Man in Old Man's Clothes', through
'The Nasal-Voiced Youth', who experimented with words
being sounds as much as they were messages, then 'The
Braying Beatnik' of 'Maggie's Farm', via 'The Country
Crooner' of 'Nashville Skyline', all the way to 'The Grizzled
Old Troubadour' of the present day. Dylan himself has admitted that this is true, writing in his book *Chronicles* that when
he recorded 'Nashville Skyline', 'The music press didn't know
what to make of it. I used a different voice too'. It made me
realise that, in fact, some singers *do* get away with altering
their voices, or experimenting with different vocal sounds;
and to do that while still persuading people that you have a
distinct and settled vocal identity is quite an achievement.)

*

ME: So when did you find your own voice?

GREEN: The 'Scritti' voice we mentioned was arrived at almost abruptly when I got sick of British indie guitar music. Abruptly, but only semi-consciously. It's a voice that returned to early 1960s white pop influences mixed with some American R 'n' B pop singing from the 1980s. For a bunch of reasons it's a voice with pretty much no vibrato. Maybe that's its distinguishing feature? I think that's because the sugary, white-bread pop music I liked as a boy was sung by men with relatively 'pure', unornamented voices. Not much wobbling going on with the Beatles or the Beach Boys, for example. Also a lot of 1960s 'countercultural' bands had singers who eschewed earlier more 'mannered' stylings. And I had a distaste for melodramatic vibrato, maybe particularly when used by white singers. Listening to contemporary black R 'n' B then coincided with becoming even more suspicious of the 'truth' of the voice and of 'expressivity'. That came in part from Derrida.

I'm so glad he mentioned Derrida. See, I told you he'd be good at talking about things like truth and authenticity; I knew he'd have thought about all this. On we go.

GREEN: I realise now too that I liked the touch of the androgynous and childlike in a voice. I found it ... or put it in my voice a little. I'm sure it's something from 'the unconscious'. It's arguably the voice of an other. It's psychic ventriloquy. I think I remember some critic saying I sang like Violet Elizabeth Bott, the spoilt girl from the *Just William* books. How perfect! He criticised me for not having the right kind of voice for singing R 'n' B. That was precisely my point.

ME: Brilliant. And, in the end, do you feel you have a good, positive relationship with your own voice, or is it complicated?

GREEN: I had a bit of an unhappy relationship with my voice. I couldn't really control it. It's still hard to control. I have no technical expertise whatsoever. My voice lacks 'wallop' or 'punch'. Maybe that has a lot to do with a lack of confidence. But then I did like Simon and Garfunkel and people like Colin Blunstone.

ME: And did you ever have singing lessons or anything?

GREEN: I had literally a couple of singing lessons in the early 1980s with a well-spoken lady in a leafy north London suburb.

ME: That was probably Tona de Brett, wasn't it? She did everyone.

GREEN: She asked me to hold her chest while she sang. I pretty much fled in embarrassment. Also I had a couple of lessons with a little old man in Manhattan who taught Liza Minelli (you can hear it, can't you?). I just did some scales and stuff. No apparent effect whatsoever.

ME: And so do you prefer studio recording or live singing?

GREEN: I like singing in the studio ... doing it till it's right. Singing live is like a complicated sporting event for the voice. A fiendish obstacle race. Over this hurdle, around this tricky bend, down for this horrible low note.

ME: This is the most brilliant description of live singing I have ever heard, and I relate to it one hundred per cent.

GREEN: It's pure concentration, and it's a great feeling when it occasionally goes well.

ME: Haha, 'occasionally'. And you suffer from stage fright?

GREEN: Stage fright stopped me singing live for twenty years. I still get horribly anxious and fuck up, but now I like gigging.

ME: You're braver than me – I haven't done a gig for fifteen years and still can't really imagine doing one.

GREEN: Just as a final thought, by the way: you make the voice more or less Scritti by constricting or relaxing some ligaments in your throat, and by varying degrees of smiling.

ME: *Hang on*, are you saying we can all do the Scritti voice, just *by smiling*?

If you are not now trying to sing 'The Sweetest Girl' while experimenting with different degrees of smiling, then you are not the reader I took you for.

9

A WINDOW PANE

I'm fascinated by the idea of the folk voice being almost invisible, or at least, that invisibility is the goal. 'Good prose should be transparent, like a window pane', wrote George Orwell, and a similar, perhaps unattainable, ideal seems true for many folk singers. The singing should always be in the service of the song; that seems to be the ultimate ambition. Bob Dylan writes about his early beginnings in *Chronicles*, 'There were a lot of better singers and better musicians around these places but there wasn't anybody close in nature to what I was doing . . . Most of the other performers tried to put themselves across, rather than the song, but I didn't care about doing that. With me, it was about putting the song across.' In traditional folk, where singers draw on a shared pool of material, it is all about interpretation, conveying the essence of the song, and much less about the beauty of the sound you might make

with your voice. Folk singing developed out of an oral tradition of storytelling; as Will Hodgkinson writes in *The
Ballad of Britain*, people sang 'to tell stories, to mark events,
to relay the news and to bring poetry to the most mundane
aspects of daily life'. He goes on to interview various
singers from the Traveller community, including Stanley
Robertson, nephew of the famed Jeannie Robertson, who
grew up in a folk-singing family. Stanley talks about how
the singer inhabits the song, becomes at one with it, and all
others who have sung and heard it: 'You're singing with a
tribe. You're a villain, you're a wronged woman, you're a
wee boy with a letter, you're everyone.' In this sense, the
singer merges with the characters in the song; his own
identity becomes subsumed into the story. This is what
Dylan is saying too, about his early singing – that it wasn't
even about trying to create and communicate a distinctive
personality; he wanted to obscure himself, and be in the
service of the songs. One of the things that make Dylan's
performances of his own topical songs work is his deadpan
delivery. He lets the lyrics and the story they tell deliver all
the feeling required, and there is no emotional demand in
his actual vocal. He sings them in a plain, almost detached
manner. Conversely, when you hear other singers cover
one of his 'angry' songs, they often believe that they have
to supply the anger in the vocals, and that is a mistake – the
songs immediately sound histrionic, and you feel hectored
and lectured in a way that you never do by Dylan's own
interpretations of his songs.

Shirley Collins reiterated this same perspective in an
interview with Jude Rogers in the *Guardian* in 2008, in

which she said, 'A folk voice should just be a conduit for the song. You want no sheen, just the song.' This idea of there being no sheen is central to folk singing, and is part of the music's ongoing debate over the tension between the real, or the natural, and the artifice of performance. Folk music has always been big on the idea of informality, and presents itself as the antithesis of pop music: simpler, more homely and authentic. It is anti-glamour, in a way that reminds me strongly of the demystification of punk and post-punk. Also, unlike at conventional pop or rock gigs, there's an attempt to break down the barrier between performer and listener; so at folk clubs there might be no stage, no amps, no dressing up, and the idea is to erase the boundary between performance and participation.

In the *Guardian* interview, Shirley Collins responds to the revived interest in folk music with ambivalence – on the one hand happy to see it being kept alive and handed down through the generations, but on the other harbouring a perhaps old-fashioned prejudice against the concept of performance. She describes certain modern singers dismissively: 'Many of them are almost turning themselves into pantomime acts. They're so self-aware, strutting around, turning it into theatre. What they should remember is that these songs are about people, not a person.' It's important, in other words, that the singer does not become the centre of attention, more important than either the listener or the people contained within the songs. It's a dilemma, for singer and listener, both of whom have to partake in something that is definitely A Show, while also buying into the notion that something entirely natural is taking place. A certain suspension of disbelief has to be adopted by both sides.

Returning to the subject of accents, this has always been something of a hot topic in folk music: the adoption of the correct accent is taken very seriously. If you're singing traditional ballads, then obviously you're not going to adopt the vague transatlantic accent of pop, so the idea of singing in your 'own' accent has long been a badge of sincerity and character. Outside the more purist circles, though, where folk blurs into the world of rock, choice of accent is a more open, more personal decision. Nick Drake, for instance, is steadfastly English, even when his songs transcend folk arrangements and veer towards commercial soulful rock, as on 'Poor Boy'. The track is loose and sensuous; a sax wails, the piano is jazzy and improvisational, the female backing vocalists are singing in an American accent, but there is Nick at the centre of it all, sounding as genteel and English as ever. It creates a tension, a slight awkwardness that saves the track from overproduced blandness, but did that awkwardness contribute to people finding his music difficult to grasp and interpret? Did that voice in the midst of that arrangement constitute something of the bizarre hybrid?

John Martyn, in contrast, sang in a more obviously US-inspired accent, and I would argue that it lent his singing some of the power and authority that an American accent often seems to imbue. An English tone like Nick Drake's, beautiful and true though it is, will always risk sounding whimsical or even fey, whereas the swaggering resonance of US pronunciation brings with it a sense of innate machismo. I think of Sinatra, and what his accent conveys – confidence, control, maturity. Sometimes, of course, an English accent can be a way of deliberately implying the exact opposite: it can add an atmosphere of amateurism, making the voice appear less professional, less showbiz, even. Lily Allen, for example, is someone whose accent lends an unstudied artlessness to her performances, making her sound youthful, a little bit street, a little bit naive, but above all, less like a Singer, and more like a person who happens to be singing. She has the strength of personality to carry it off, but with an English accent you tread a fine line between simple and twee; and the desperate desire to avoid the namby-pamby, whimsical aspects of indie was another reason why I veered towards an American accent at the beginning of my career. No one singing in an American accent will ever sound twee as someone singing in English can.

Still, it's a risk. Alexis Petridis, reviewing Laura Marling's album *Once I Was an Eagle* in the *Guardian*, raised an eyebrow at the recent Americanisation of her accent, highlighting the fact that it had reached a point where she was pronouncing the word 'verse' in pure Brooklyn-ese, as 'voice'. Too much obvious deviation from an accent you've established will be seen as insincerity. But it depends too on the kind of music you're singing – we were fine with the idea that Joss Stone, performing entirely American-inspired music, was singing in that accent, and it wasn't until she forgot herself for a moment and started *speaking* in it that ridicule loomed. That was considered a step too far and made her look foolish – and it's noteworthy as an example of how clearly we distinguish between singing and speaking voice in terms of what's acceptable.

An alternative way to avoid this pitfall is to use a regional accent, if you happen to be in possession of one. The Proclaimers did so in the most decisive fashion, securing for themselves a unique sound identity above and beyond anything in their actual songs. And two of my favourite singers of recent years, Rachel and Becky Unthank, sing in the Tyne and Wear voices they were born with, loud and proud. It's a gorgeous sound, warm and earthy, and lends a sort of stoic muscularity to anything they sing. Again, there is a complete absence of twee. For the listener, though, singing along becomes problematic: if, like me, you're someone for whom one of the prime enjoyments of music is the singing along, then accents can throw obstacles in your path, making you feel awkward and inhibited. Do you sing in your own, probably vaguely American singing voice, or join in with the particular accent being used? If you do the latter, you risk sounding like you're taking the piss.

And what about emotion and passion within the folk scenario of ordinariness? Is there room for any soul or self in the folk voice, and is there even meant to be? If the idea is that it's all about conveying the song in the most honest, direct, authentic way possible, rather than using the song as a vehicle to express the self; that discovering unknown old songs is of more value than writing new ones, in that there is a buried tradition, which speaks volumes about our heritage, our past and where we come from, and that the singer's duty is to learn and faithfully reproduce these songs, then is there a danger that the singing of these songs can become an almost mechanical process? Does it reduce the singer to a mere cog in the machine?

Possibly, though I can think of many folk singers who defy this apparent ban on performance and personality. At its best, the folk voice encompasses the deadpan neutrality of Anne Briggs and the regal imperiousness of Sandy Denny, both of which I find packed with an unshowy, austere kind of emotion. In folk singing, the worst thing you can be is a bit fake, a bit pop, a bit showbiz. 'Just sing it straight' is the mantra, the apparent opposite of soul singing, with its ad-libs, vibrato and melisma. Folk singing strains towards the minimal, whereas soul singers so often seek to add, whether in the form of Aretha Franklin's swoops of extended range, James Brown's grunts of sexual exertion, or the likes of Luther Vandross and Mariah Carey who simply include as many notes as possible in each sung phrase. Sometimes, at its worst, the result comes across as simply showing off, but in the secure hands of the best singers you get a performance akin to that of an Olympic athlete, which leaves you breathless in admiration of its almost superhuman skill and ability. I'm reminded of Simon Frith describing Whitney Houston 'swinging through a ballad like a trapeze artist'. Sometimes that's just what you want. You can't always have it sung plain; the ear needs treats and sweets some of the time. One of the few soul singers who does sing it straight is Sade, and while some dismiss her lack of range and versatility, others are delighted by her firm, almost prim refusal to overdo things, to be vulgar, to risk making a mess.

I inhabit a territory somewhere in the plainsong world of the folk voice, which rarely intersects with soul singing; and yet some people like to describe me as a soul or jazz singer. I've borrowed mannerisms and inflections from both sides, but essentially I'm a lyric-delivering kind of singer, a teller of the story, not an embellisher. Folk singing eschews vibrato and ad-libs, and I'm not strong on those. If I have any vibrato at all, it's not soul vibrato, but closer to the deliberate note-wobble of someone like Chrissie Hynde, whose voice has always reminded me of the tremolo setting on a guitar amp – something added to the note rather than contained within it. And if I'm jazzy, then it's the little corner table of Blossom Dearie and Astrud Gilberto that I'm sitting at, with singers whose economy of style, direct- ness of delivery and absence of flourish I share. Singing is in many ways an elevated or enhanced form of speaking, and this particular style is aiming to be not *too* enhanced. If singing makes us hear, open up and be receptive to the emotion contained within words, it is also true that beyond a certain point singing can become so florid as to draw more attention to itself than to the words being sung, and that is a different kind of singing altogether – one I don't have much time for.

Somewhere beyond me, though, out past the rather modest vocal territory where I dwell, there is a realm I gaze at enviously, where Dusty soars above me and Björk reaches levels I can't. My style of singing suits me, and sits with my personality, but still, I'd love to be Adele for a day.

10

LOOKS LIKE AN ELEPHANT

I've mentioned several times the importance of finding your own voice, and the recurring arguments focused on artifice and faking it. The most literal examples of this involve not the singer who puts on a different voice in which to sing, or gives a mannered performance, but the instances of actual fakery with which pop music is littered. In fact, the potential for deception existed right from the beginning of recording technology, and was recognised early, seeming to some to offer a solution to certain perceived problems. Greg Milner, in *Perfecting Sound Forever*, tells the story of pioneering orchestra conductor Leopold Stokowski, who engaged in some of the earliest attempts to record an orchestra in the late 1920s, and is quoted as saying this: 'Opera today, while pleasing to the ear, is often a sore trial for the eye. Take Tannhäuser, for example. Venus, the most beautiful woman in the world, is using her charms to tempt Tannhäuser from the narrow path of virtue. But, unfortunately, the lady who plays the part . . . may sing like a nightingale, but she looks like an elephant . . . Electricity will change her. We can take her voice and record it on a disk. Then we can select a beautiful young lady who really may be accepted by the audience for a Venus . . . '

The sheer brutality and sexism of this suggestion is bracing in its straightforwardness and its clear belief that here is a simple solution to a problem that we can all agree upon. It sets out the case for faking the lead singer, and as with most technological advances, once it becomes possible to do something, it is perhaps inevitable that sooner or later someone will do it. The moral implications don't seem to have troubled Stokowski for a moment, though as it turned out, they *would* trouble the paying public, who would prove bitterly resentful of this kind of deceit when it was practised upon them. Taking for granted that any audience would rather listen to a beautiful young lady than one who 'looks like an elephant', Stokowski merely anticipated the trend of popular music, which would make it ever more difficult for female singers to sidestep the question of their appearance, and be judged solely on the quality of their singing. Within the world of commercial pop music it became obvious that it would be easier to sell a record 'sung' by a conventionally attractive woman, and so the temptation was there to commit the ultimate act of vocal artifice. One of the most notorious examples is that of Black Box, who sampled Loleatta Holloway's voice on their hit 'Ride on Time', and on other releases used vocals they had recorded from Martha Wash, while claiming the model who lip-synched the vocals in 'live' performances and videos was the group's real lead singer. Or maybe they never 'claimed' any such thing, maybe they just didn't think it really mattered, believing, like Stokowski, that the jarring disconnect between a beautiful voice coming from a 'not beautiful' body was too upsetting to impose on an audience, and that they were merely fixing things to make it nicer for everybody.

To prove that this kind of fakery wasn't only a sexist conspiracy against women, one of the other more famous examples involves men. Two men, in fact; the men who were or weren't Milli Vanilli. Their story and their controversy is well known – they were disgraced and had their Grammy revoked after it was revealed that the group members Fab Morvan and Rob Pilatus had not been the ones singing on their record or indeed at their concerts, where they were miming to the vocal performances of others. The public reaction that followed demonstrates that, in fact, people *do* think it matters who is claiming to be the singer; that there is a fundamental issue of integrity, which the record-buying public take seriously. After the Milli Vanilli revelations, members of the public filed lawsuits against the group demanding refunds. This is curious, of course, because while it's indisputable that there was deception happening, if people had bought and enjoyed the records, they didn't really lose anything once it was revealed that different people had been doing the singing. The record they liked was still the same record, still sounded exactly the way it had the previous day. Indeed, those who perhaps had the most right to feel aggrieved were the singers who actually performed the songs, only to see others claim all the credit and rewards. Nonetheless, it's a fact that the public felt they had been defrauded. It seems that there is a bond of trust between those selling and those buying records – the voice has to belong to the person you have been led to believe it belongs to, or else you have been conned and deprived of the true experience you thought you were paying for.

It turns out that the public can get irate about vocal authenticity even when it's not an instance of one person pretending to be another, but of a singer – Beyoncé, perhaps – lip-synching to a performance she herself had previously recorded, at a presidential inauguration, say. I was taken aback by the controversy over the Obama inauguration. The situation was explained pretty quickly – a vocal had been pre-recorded as a safety copy in case of technical issues, and then lack of rehearsal time with the orchestra, combined with a strong wind on the day, or something, made them decide to go with the pre-record and not risk any musical dissonance at such a large and important public event. Didn't sound very controversial to me. Was anyone actually suggesting that Beyoncé herself hadn't sung the pre-recorded vocal? Or, and here I may have to pause for a moment to laugh, that Beyoncé *can't sing*? That she's been faking it all this time and she's no better than Milli Vanilli? We need to have a quiet word with ourselves here if we have gone down this path of thinking. Those arguing that the avoidance of a risk that this particular musical performance might go awry was a bad thing, and that Beyoncé should be ashamed of herself for her artistic cowardice, should take a moment to remember that this was not a concert, or indeed a musical event of any kind. It was a symbolic, wholly stage-managed piece of state pageantry, and the singing was absolutely not the central event. What this story proved to me, though, was that people can still get agitated about the idea that what they are getting is not what they signed up for.

On the subject of hidden singers, no one exemplifies this phenomenon better than Marni Nixon, who sang the vocals for many lead actresses in musical films, often receiving neither credit nor proper royalties for her efforts. She sang the high notes Marilyn Monroe couldn't reach, and was dubbed over Deborah Kerr's singing voice in *The King and I* and Audrey Hepburn's in *My Fair Lady*. Perhaps most notoriously, when she sang Natalie Wood's part of Maria in *West Side Story*, the fact was apparently kept secret even from the actress herself. Denied a full royalty payment by the film's producers, she ended up receiving a portion of Leonard Bernstein's royalty, so at least someone recognised that this practice came too close to being both exploitative and disreputable.

From the singer's point of view, acknowledgement and recognition are understandably important – no one wants to do all the work only for someone else to take all the credit. In my experience, however, 'hidden' singing can sometimes be a satisfying experience, a way of deflecting the limelight and getting to enjoy taking part without having to shoulder the full responsibility of representing the work. At various points in my career, making guest appearances or singing backing vocals with other artists has performed this function for me, opened up opportunities and given me the chance to flit in and out of people's music – not uncredited, no, but unburdened in some way, not having to be The Lead Singer who is the focus of attention. When I sang with The Style Council on 'The Paris Match' I was a virtually unknown singer, my fame and status way below that of Paul Weller. The credits on the album artwork were sketchy, so that for years many people muddled me up with Tracie Young, who had sung backing vocals with The Jam and then sang on the first Style Council single, 'Speak Like a Child'. I didn't really mind this; it was a way of being invisible, heard but not seen. I carried on with my guest appearances, singing with Working Week on 'Venceremos', then doing backing vocals for The Go-Betweens and Lloyd Cole. There's a joy to singing backing vocals, whether on your own or other people's records; it's where singing becomes not an art, but a craft; not about expressiveness, but about accuracy. Layering harmonies requires precision of pitch, but also subtleties of vocal pronunciation. You have to moderate the sibilance of your 's's, de-emphasise explosive consonants, allow words to tail off with no conclusion so that the word endings don't all land in slightly different places. These skills only come with experience and practice, and there's a satisfaction in learning them.

I sang a jazzy version of 'Over the Rainbow' with trumpet player James McMillan, and a drum and bass song with Adam F. I sang trip-hop with Massive Attack, and deep house with Tiefschwarz and then Tevo Howard. A gorgeous yearning ballad with The Unbending Trees. I probably brought a lot of myself and my own sound to all those performances, but still, they each offered a kind of escape route from being *me*, a liberation from being the one whose face and name was in bold type on the sleeve, a way of appearing and disappearing at the same time. For me, there were certain consolations to being the hidden singer, or perhaps I should say partly hidden. And perhaps it's only when you practise complete concealment that you run into problems.

Another example of people feeling tricked by singers can be seen in the upset and outrage which whirls around the use of Auto-Tune. The general public first became aware of it in 1998, when it was used on Cher's track 'Believe' to create that robotic vocal effect you either love or hate. That was the year I began to creep into a form of retirement, so it's fair to say that me and Auto-Tune, we passed in the night. Then again, I've made records since then, and I'd be lying if I claimed that no studio technology had ever been used on my vocal to make the odd correction. It's controversial, though, and while I can understand why, I'm still struck by people's misconceptions about how and when it is used, and what it's good for.

The story of recording vocals in the studio is one where the apparently competing claims of authenticity and artifice are played out over and over. Debates about how to capture a sound that is most 'real', most truly reflective of the actual sound being produced by the person singing, have raged since microphones were invented and recording began. Different microphones capture sound in different ways, and therefore will make a vocal sound dissimilar, but which is more true to life? Some would argue that the most realistic capturing of the human voice is still created by singing into a horn and recording direct onto a wax cylinder, something that has not been the norm for a very long time. So have we simply got used to listening to distorted or inauthentic reproductions of vocals?

Adding echo, or reverb, to a vocal can enhance the sound, increasing the listener's enjoyment, but is it authentic? You may be singing in a tiny corner of the studio, but with that particular reverb setting you are now performing in a great hall, and I don't think I've ever heard anyone complain about that as being deceptive or fake.

You might contend that it's the overuse of Auto-Tune, not its use in principle, that has led to protests against it. When Jay-Z rapped on 'D.O.A. (Death of Auto-Tune)' that 'This is anti-Auto-Tune', I guess he was making an argument for a return to roughness and realness, in which case he has a point. But when writer Neil McCormick called Auto-Tune a 'particularly sinister invention' that operates by taking 'a poorly sung note and . . . placing it dead centre of where it was meant to be' I have to take issue with that melodramatic and moralising word 'sinister'. Bizarrely for a piece of recording studio gadgetry, it was included in a *Time* magazine list of 'The 50 Worst Inventions', a list that you can only hope prioritised things like nukes and drones over a plug-in that can slightly pitch-bend a sung note of music.

Much of the controversy around it seems misguided and misinformed to me, and muddles up the artistic use of

Auto-Tune – as in Cher's 'Believe', and then countless other pop and dance tracks, which turn it into an audible, deliberate feature of the track – with plain overuse, as happens in too much current pop recording. If you're not sure what I mean by overuse, you can quickly acquaint yourself with the sound by popping on a *Glee* album. I watched the early series of *Glee* and was a big fan of its gloriously camp celebration of the notion that pop music can still be the saviour of high school outsiders. But Lord, after a while the Auto-Tune nearly killed me, and there is nothing that compares to the experience of listening to a *Glee* album. When music snobs invented the dismissive phrase 'bubblegum pop' years ago, they had no notion of how sugary and toothachey pop music might eventually become. The *Glee* recordings are surely the end point of this, the aural equivalent of the fate of Augustus Gloop. Every note has a plastic twang to it, an android quality, and it is that robotic element – so likeable when robotic is the desired effect – which turns people against Auto-Tune.

There's a kind of fierce accuracy to a heavily Auto-Tuned record, a perfection that is impossible to achieve naturally, and so it renders the sound superhuman, and as a consequence, less than human. Flaws embody qualities like warmth, approachability, connection – easily lost when all the flaws are removed, as in an airbrushed photo. But to be completely anti is to misunderstand how Auto-Tune is used when it's used 'properly'. It's almost as though critics believe that Auto-Tune is a kind of topping, which you smear all over a track like whipped cream, burying everything authentic, smothering the music in a glossy, rich coating. But this isn't how it has to be. In the right, judicious hands, it is simply another piece of convenient studio gadgetry.

And if you think you hate Auto-Tune, that implies you can always detect when it has been used, in which case you have magic ears and can be very proud of yourself. Many modern pop records are homogenously and obviously Auto-Tuned, yes, but the fact is that other artists use it carefully and you would never ever know. Sometimes even the artist themselves might never be aware of it, as in the case of a producer I know who worked with a singer who was otherwise great but had a tendency to wander on the tuning. When she was out of the studio, he and the engineer would apply the 'magic compressor' to her vocal. She'd come back in and be thrilled at how they had improved things just with some basic studio technology. The word Auto-Tune was never mentioned. Everyone was happy. I would put money on the fact that you heard that record and never guessed.

The ideal application is for the correction of a single note in an otherwise good performance. The alternative to Auto-Tune in the old days – and I'm old enough to remember this, and what a drag it was – was that you had to 'drop in' in order to correct a bum note. You wouldn't want to sing the whole song again, or even necessarily the whole verse, when only one line has a mistake in it, and there's something in the take that you don't want to lose – a great tone of voice, an emotional moment, a strength, a vulnerability – but having to sing one or two words is awkward. You sing the whole line in order to run up to it so it sounds natural, but the engineer has to go into, and then out of, record at *exactly* the right moment. Sometimes he misses; you have to do it again. Sometimes you miss the note a second time, and you have to go again. Again and again. It can kill performance, mood, emotion. It can be the opposite of the authentic performance, in fact the most artificial way to record a vocal. Some singers with anxiety issues or studio phobias could end up piecing together takes from a line here, a word there. It's hardly a true representation of a vocal performance, and proves nothing about who is a 'better' singer. That was in the Proper Old Days. Nowadays, things are easier, and when you record using software like Pro Tools, it's very easy to re-sing sections of a song and then piece together the best bits; there's no need for old-skool 'dropping in'. Still, you have to be able to hit that problematic note, and that might still mean singing the line over and over. Auto-Tune, or any of its current equivalents – a clever human invention, just as anaesthetics and refrigeration are – can be used to make adjustments here and there, salvaging all that is valuable in a particular performance for our benefit and enjoyment.

Like most things, though, there is a time and a place for it. At the poppier end of the spectrum, records can strain towards a clean, perfect sound, and can thrill us with their aspiration, their ambition, their sheer upward mobility. Other records will always revel in, and thrill us with their imperfections. In the end, the whole debate asks us one simple question: what do we want from singers? And the answer has to be, we don't always want or need the same things – and what the listener wants is not always what the singer wants. *Time* journalist Josh Tyrangiel called Auto-Tune 'Photoshop for the human voice'. And if we could Photoshop some of our own holiday snaps, would we not sometimes choose to do so? My first solo album, *A Distant Shore*, was one of my earliest attempts at studio singing, and contains 'pitchy' moments. So if I could go back and Auto-Tune a few of those notes, potentially sacrificing some of the authenticity, but also fixing notes that make me wince, would I? Oh, you bet your life I would.

11

RUFUS WAINWRIGHT'S TROUSERS

For some, the claim that a voice is at least in part a constructed or 'chosen' thing will always be anathema, and they will cling to the romantic image of the artist as possessed of instinctive, natural talent. Willa Cather's *The Song of the Lark* dramatises the push and pull between these two concepts, and different notions of what a singer is, or should be. The novel raises questions about how a singer finds their voice, where that voice comes from, and what role intelligence or conscious thought plays in the act of singing, and in distinguishing good singing from bad. You can see how a writer might be interested in this idea, and want to explore or even debunk the notion that an effortless connection between singer and listener, or between writer and reader, is either possible or desirable.

The Song of the Lark tells the story of Thea Kronborg, who grows up in a small desert town of the American west, discovers a strong connection with music as a child, and then later is found to have a unique singing voice which leads her to fame and fortune, but at the expense of family ties and personal relationships. At first glance, it is an archetypally romantic portrait of the artist as someone with superior gifts, an almost childlike sense of wonder at the world, and a sense that they are only truly themselves through the discovery and exploration of their art.

As a child, Thea is slow to speak – 'inept in speech' despite her intelligence – as if her speaking voice is somehow imprisoned within her; the voice is something precious, not to be given away too freely, or too soon. Her first teacher is Wunsch, an elderly musician who drinks, and he is the first to detect her particular talents – he feels that the beauty of her voice is innate, and its quality is present even when she reads the lyrics of German lieder he teaches her: 'It was a nature-voice ... and apart from language.' He is the first in the book to propound the argument that is a central theme – that artistic talent is something one is born with: 'Some things cannot be taught ... For a singer there must be something in the inside from the beginning.'

Thea herself is aware of a feeling that is beyond her conscious control, and it ebbs and flows, fluid and intangible. She likes to sing with the local Mexicans, who live in the poor part of town and are looked down upon; in her bond with them, the implication is that she has 'soul', and that they, as a more primitive people, are still in touch with the spirituality of music, a quality which Thea shares. This motif occurs too in *Daniel Deronda*, where Mirah's Jewishness also seems intended to imply that she has a special connection to the realm of artistry and spirituality. By our modern standards, this is uncomfortable stereotyping, endowing other races or nationalities with innate gifts, suggesting that they are 'other' – dark, mysterious and primal. Nonetheless, it's an idea about singers that persists, that some are more possessed of natural emotion, and this quality is what raises one singer above another. In the novel, Thea's piano teacher Harsanyi believes that not only is the voice natural, but that it is separate from the singer's consciousness – innate, beyond her control: 'All the intelligence and talent in the world can't make a singer. The voice is a wild thing. It can't be bred in captivity. It is a sport, like the silver fox.'

Thea, on the other hand, believes differently, and this is what makes the story thought-provoking. She knows that singing is more than pure emotion, and as her success grows, she becomes increasingly resentful of the notion that singing is not governed by intelligence, or skill, or hard work, and of some of the idiocies she encounters in other singers. 'Singing doesn't seem to be a very brainy profession,' she says. She plays piano as accompanist to fellow singers Mrs Priest and Jessie Darcey, and finds their lack of technique and the crudeness of their crowd-pleasing antics infuriating. Their success infuriates her even more, making her question the level of intelligence in the audience – 'But people seemed to like Jessie Darcey exactly because she could not sing; because, as they put it, she was "so natural and unprofessional." Her singing was pronounced "artless," her voice "bird-like."' Thea is aware that artifice, and skill, are an essential part of good singing, and that the adulation of the natural is mere vulgarity and shallowness on the part of the audience.

We are back to the question of authenticity versus artificiality, and of what value to place upon singing. If it is simply a natural gift, can the singer be regarded as an artist? If art is all about vision and choice, and how the artist shapes his or her material in order to present it to the world, then to emphasise the innate qualities of the singer is to devalue her. As an aside, it's worth remembering that not only are singers often not regarded as artists, they are sometimes not even regarded as musicians. In the 1920s and 1930s, the early crooners had to hold an instrument, even a fake instrument, as it was inconceivable that you could just be a singer and do nothing else. Bing Crosby, for example, was given a violin with rubber strings to pose with. Similarly, up until 1979 singers were not eligible to join the American Federation of Musicians, but had to apply for membership as a player of some instrument or other. So it's no exaggeration to talk about the downgrading of singing compared to other forms of musical expression.

Thea stands up, in no uncertain terms, for the right of the singer to claim her status as artist, and the presence of intelligence is central to her perception of what makes a good artist. Without it, all you have is a basic talent that cannot go beyond the ordinary. The belief that audiences can't always tell the difference between the good and the bad is commonplace among musicians and performers, and at its worst it smacks of arrogance, of contempt for the people who have paid to witness the performance. But we should recall that there can be distinct things going on inside the head of the singer and the head of the listener: sometimes the connection between the two can feel strong, but at other times they are worlds apart.

I have often found this myself. When I started singing, I didn't think twice about what was happening during a gig, or what I and everyone around me was feeling. Usually gigs were short, and small, so that you were close to the crowd, and could easily believe that you were all sharing the same experience. But as my career progressed, and the gigs got bigger, I became aware of the distance between the stage and the auditorium, and began to notice that, in fact, maybe the experiences of the band and the crowd were quite different. For instance, at a concert, a singer may perform an emotional song while being actually very detached from the emotion. The listener, however, perceives the presence of strong emotion – so who has put it there? If the singer isn't conscious of feeling anything at the time, and is even potentially just going through the motions, is emotion really present or is the listener imagining it? The audience's emotional response is often determined as much by the memories the song evokes as by the performance taking place – you hear a song and are transported back to the first time you heard it, or a period in your life when you listened to it a lot. Maybe it was with someone you loved, it was 'your' song; maybe they're here with you now, maybe – even worse – they're not. There is a wealth of your own personal meaning encoded within the song, and in a way, the singer is completely extraneous to the experience you're having.

They might not even sing it very well – does it matter, will you notice? Does it just need to be 'good enough' to trigger the responses that are really contained entirely within *you*? In *A Singer's Notebook* Ian Bostridge touches on the relationship between feeling and performance, and relates this story: 'I shall never forget a masterclass in which one of my fellow students proudly moved himself to tears with his own performance. The distinguished teacher's response was cruel but salutary: "Don't worry, dear. It wasn't all that bad."' The point being that the singer's feelings at the moment of performance are largely irrelevant. The emotion should already be there, in the song itself, and you felt it at the moment you wrote the song – you shouldn't need to relive it every time you perform.

On stage, it is hard not to be distracted by external concerns. There are practical and prosaic thoughts going through our heads, 'noise' which has to be ignored, as far as that is ever possible. What we hope is that none of it is apparent to the audience. But having been on the stage myself, as an audience member I often find it a challenge to become as immersed in live gigs as I know others do. I am too aware of what's going on up there and the range of things that might actually be happening. A few years ago I saw Rufus Wainwright doing a solo show at Islington Academy, and it reminded me of the incredible intensity and intimacy of the acoustic performance; the up-close connection with the real performer right there in front of you. And the audience may be having a uniquely spiritual experience, but for the performer there is a never-ending stream of interferences from the outside physical world, which threaten to disrupt. When I got home from the gig I wrote in my diary:

Rufus is wearing shiny red trousers, which make him slither around a little on the barstool when he sits to play guitar. He jokes about it, but it's probably irritating him. Funny how the decision of which trousers to wear can have an impact on your performance. They look great in the dressing room mirror, but now, on stage, they're being a nuisance. Your ability to concentrate and emote is being let down by your choice of trousers. And the in-ear monitors keep falling out, like they always do. Halfway through his version of "Hallelujah", he repeats himself. "Have I sung this verse already?" he sings, in the middle of a verse that he is indeed repeating. The audience laughs, loving this moment of human frailty. I bet he just drifted off for a moment. Maybe he's sung this song too many times? Is he thinking of something else entirely? The next song, maybe, or the uncomfortable level in his monitors? Or the slippery trousers?

Most, if not all, of the audience would have been unaware of these issues, and have probably never noticed or wondered what the experience is like for the singer up on the stage. And often, of course, the audience doesn't recognise elements of performance which are particularly good or, on the other hand, haven't quite worked. As the performer, this can make you feel that your efforts are wasted or meaningless, and that the live show is something that both matters and doesn't matter. For a sufferer from stage fright, the event is built up to a size that is out of proportion to its actual importance: it matters *too much*. But then, if the audience doesn't relate to the performance in a way that feels true – i.e. mistakes are not noticed, cliches are treated as high points – then the meaning contained in the music can seem devalued. There is endless decision-making involved in producing music: what to do, how to do it, how to judge when something is good and finished. But there can sometimes be a gulf between performer and audience, which makes the performer feel disconnected from their listeners, or worst of all, contemptuous of them. Singers can learn tricks which please an audience, which always work and get a response, but can then despise the audience for falling for those tricks, or failing to notice the more subtle moments which have taken real skill or imagination.

In all this distraction and stagecraft, what happens to the spiritual element, the transcendent moment that is the whole reason the audience is there? Perhaps, in truth, the spiritual connection is really created by the listeners, who are engaged in as much of a creative act as the singer, producing from within themselves a wealth of emotions, memories, significances. Making clear how intrinsic a part of the musical experience it is, how much of a collaborative act, Wayne Koestenbaum brings the act of listening vividly to life when he writes: 'A singer's voice sets up vibrations and resonances in the listener's body. First, there are the physiological sensations we call "hearing". Second, there are gestures of response with which the listener mimics the singer, expresses physical sympathy, appreciation, or exaltation: shudder, gasp, sigh; holding the body motionless, relaxing the shoulders, stiffening the spine.

'Listening, your heart is in your throat: *your* throat, not the diva's.'

Truly, then, it is the listener who is the one most in possession of what we call 'feeling' at this point. The sound enters the listener and a physical and mental − chemical, even − process takes place, at the end of which something entirely new has been created. The listener believes the singer has done it, and that they have passively received what has been offered, but in reality both parties are involved, and the listener − who can make anything happen: transform a lacklustre performance into the night of their life, be lifted to the heavens by a singer who is going through the motions on a weekday gig halfway through a long tour − is even more vital than the singer.

In Arthur Phillips's novel, *The Song Is You*, there is a good description of the relationship between the singer and the listener − a music fan listens to a singer he loves, and the songs connect with him, as if they understand him, and 'when the song was working' it feels as though there were 'a unique two-way connection between his mind and that voice, which must therefore be aware of him'. This is a good insight into how and why we feel so close to the singers we love − the delusion that the flow of understanding and knowing goes both ways; that the feelings engendered in our hearts, or brains, when we hear a song, can actually be experienced in return by the singer; that we know them, and they know us in return; that the feeling is mutual.

*

Sometimes there is simply no place for emotion on stage; there is too much else going on, and so its presence is left to chance. It can be interrupted and disrupted by other goings-on in the room, even by the behaviour of the audience. Whatever kind of line-up we were touring with, whether a small electric combo, a larger band with a horn section, or later a more electronic set-up with programmed drums and synths, we would often end gigs with an acoustic encore, just me singing and Ben on guitar, where we'd perform something like 'Fascination'. I'd be more relaxed by this point, the gig almost over, anxieties beginning to recede, a feeling of the shoulders dropping; and because of this it would often be the moment when I was most aware of the emotion in a song, and 'Fascination' was one that spoke to me, and to audiences, very clearly. When I sang it I often had the sense of something almost tangible happening and being shared, but – and here's the problem – almost as often, I had the impression that the feeling, fragile and fleeting as it was, was under threat from some audience members, who were perhaps not so caught up in the moment, were getting ready to leave, chatting, bustling, making just enough noise to intrude. It would be exasperating, and more than once it resulted in an irritable, short-tempered performance of a heartfelt, vulnerable song. I would curse myself for being distracted and rattled by a few people in the crowd, but it was inevitable once I had allowed myself to start feeling emotional on stage. The only way to avoid that kind of situation is to stay detached, calm, professional, and I'm not sure that's always what we want. It's just important to realise that live performance is a relatively uncontrolled environment, and you can't predict what will happen, either musically or emotionally.

For me, far more often the moment of emotional release is at the point of writing a song and then singing it, either inside my head or out loud for the first few times. It gives me the sense that I've come across something. It's a secret, no one else has heard it yet – and maybe they won't, if it doesn't get finished. But singing it the first few times, that's quite a rare and strange experience. You're not singing a song you've learned, or copied, or heard on the radio – you're just making it up. No one knows how it goes! You have to decide. That is the moment when you create, or uncover, or recall the emotion of the song, which you then simply have to enact every other time you perform it. I have learned over the years that I can make people cry by singing a song, and I too can be brought to tears by listening to another singer's performance. But I can't make *myself* cry with my song, nor would I want to. That would require a kind of surrender that would threaten the very coherence of any performance. After all, *someone* has to be in control here or we're all going to drown. But the moment of writing a song, coming up with a line that encapsulates everything you intend, that can be emotional, embodying both the feeling you are striving to articulate, and the satisfaction of doing so.

However, if I've implied that I am a detached and over-critical audience member, I should also confess that there are moments when I'm as drawn in as everyone else, and completely forget to wonder what else is going on beside the songs I'm hearing. A while ago, Ben made his first live solo appearance in about thirty years in the basement venue of a London pub, the Slaughtered Lamb. For the first time in all those years I was in the position of being in front of the stage that Ben was on, and while you might imagine that my familiarity with Ben, and with his style and methods of working would make me over-aware and unable simply to enjoy the music, in fact the opposite was true. I was completely absorbed, and registered only things like the change in his voice, which has grown deeper, more resonant, and somehow easier. An earlier reedy quality seems to have vanished, along with any strain or exertion, leaving a beautiful, flowing resonance and an incredible warmth to his sound. He sang for an hour and a half, and here's what struck me most: in all that time *he never had a drink of water*. Me, with all my neuroses about losing my voice, becoming too dry or having to clear my throat, I would have been sipping water after the first song, and reaching for cups of tea by the halfway point, but no, he didn't pause once. And what I assumed, because of the strength and fluidity of the performance, was that he was completely free of nerves or angst about his voice, and immersed in the moment and the singing of the songs. I had fallen into the audience trap of seeing only what was apparent, so when we got home later I was astonished to hear him tell me how nervous he'd been, how sure he was that his nerves were showing. 'There were a couple of moments,' he said, 'when I found myself thinking, "Wonder what Tracey thought of that phrasing . . . " or "Oh look, there's Geoff Travis's glasses."'

I'm just like you. I never noticed.

12

NAKED AT THE ALBERT HALL

'The attraction of the virtuoso for the public is
very like that of the circus for the crowd. There is
always the hope that something dangerous will
happen.'

Claude Debussy

Stage fright sounds like an intangible, nebulous condition. Perhaps akin to fear of spiders, or of the dark; one
of those slightly vague, purely psychological conditions,
the irrational fear of something that can't possibly hurt
you.

And in a sense, it is that – an internalised anxiety about
the thought of a bad thing happening which, in real terms,
isn't really very bad at all – a poor performance? Singing out
of tune? Forgetting words? Pah. Cry-baby. Or perhaps these
anxieties are a cover for the real heart of the fear, which

encompasses more primal, more universal feelings like the
fear of exposure, revelation, inadequacy. Or perhaps it's even
simpler than that – just the fear of not being liked. Standing
up in front of an audience, with all the audacity and arrogance that implies; imposing yourself upon them, and then
not coming up to scratch. And the audience, they will be
judging you, you know that. You've been to concerts yourself, after all; you know what you say to the person next to
you as the performance unfolds. You don't hold back, and
why should you? You've paid for this experience, and if it
doesn't deliver, you're going to say so. Up on stage, you can
imagine that verdict being delivered, and in bad moments
you see it in every audience exchange, every shared word.
It has struck countless performers, is no respecter of talent
or ability, and can either be all-encompassing, or ebb and
flow even during the course of a performance. Dusty
Springfield, in an interview with Mick Brown for the
Telegraph magazine in 1995, was quoted as describing how
just in the process of moving from one side of the stage to
the other, she could completely destabilise herself, thinking,
'I've gained confidence, I've lost it, gained it, lost it. And it's
just . . . exhausting'.

In nightmares the fear reveals itself in almost comically
obvious ways – you're on stage, but with the wrong band!
You don't know any of the songs, or any of the words! The
music begins, and you try to sing but no sound will come
out! Or, my favourite, a nightmare I actually had: I'm on
stage at the Royal Albert Hall, in the middle of a concert
that is going well, when I look down at myself and realise
I am completely naked. No real need for Dr Freud to spend

long analysing that one, you might think. You fear being exposed, do you? Thank you. Next.

On the other hand, stage fright can be built on entirely rational, comprehensible foundations. For me, the twin problems of volume and stamina lay at the root of many of my anxieties. I talked in *Bedsit Disco Queen* about the psychological aspects of my stage fright – the dislike of being looked at, and being the centre of attention. Aside from this fundamental issue, however, there were genuine physical barriers to surmount, which no amount of confidence-building or reliance on self-belief could alter. Simply put, I don't sing loud enough for live performance in anything other than a purely acoustic setting. My voice with one guitar or a piano – fine. Anything bigger in terms of arrangement and it becomes a struggle to amplify my voice enough for it to be clearly heard above the band. Audiences might imagine that it's simply a case of the sound engineer turning up the vocal on his mixing desk. Indeed, shouts of 'Turn the vocals up!', which at a couple of problematic concerts of ours were aimed in his direction, prove that there clearly are those who think there's an obvious solution and the sound engineer must be deaf, or an idiot, not to be dealing with it. What they don't seem to realise is that mixing live sound is a delicate juggling act – to have the band up loud enough to create energy and excitement in the room while keeping the lead singer audible – and there are limits to how far you can push the volume of any one ingredient without risking feedback. If the sound being produced from the stage is of a low volume, there is simply not much going into the mixing desk, and however much you crank up the controls, that vocal will only ever reach a certain level. Push it any harder and all you will create is a wall of howling feedback, which, while desirable in some circumstances, is not generally what EBTG fans paid to experience. So if the vocal has a maximum volume, the only other way to maintain balance is to turn the band *down*, thus reducing their power and impact – you can hear the vocal clearly, but the overall effect is polite, contained, limited. That's the volume problem, and it in turn created the stamina problem – in order to try to increase the decibels, I had to sing as strongly as possible, and the vocal stamina required to do that was exhausting and put strain on my voice, which could be hard to sustain over the course of a tour.

Now, add to that another physical limitation – as I mentioned earlier, I am asthmatic, not badly so, but enough that every winter I am susceptible to the slightest cold turning into a chesty cough, which lingers and rattles around for weeks. Touring's not a healthy lifestyle, made up as it is of late nights, poor diet and travel that exposes you to a menacing and ever-changing cocktail of germs, so generally within a week or two I would go down with a cold. Sore throats could sometimes be sung through, but if it went to my chest, that was that, gigs cancelled. I'd be anxious and fretful about my state of health much of the time, alarmed by every tickle in the throat, every sniffle that might be the start of something. Trying to soldier on became a constant feature of touring life. Remedies offered reflected the personality and preferences of the location. In hippy San Francisco I was offered a kind of blossom tea – dried-up pods plunged into boiling water, which bloomed like tiny lilies, producing an apparently voice-saving, though pond-flavoured potion. In more pragmatic parts of the world a doctor would be summoned to administer a nameless injection, which gave enough of a boost to get me through a two-hour show. Once, a doctor came to my hotel room and decided to give me a shot of penicillin. My body chose this moment to develop its penicillin allergy, and by the time the doctor had got back into the lift I was succumbing to an anaphylactic reaction. Luckily Ben caught him before he got out of the swing doors at reception and he returned swiftly to give me a hydrocortisone injection. I don't think I got on stage that night, but it certainly wasn't for want of trying. Cancelling gigs cost money and goodwill, and was to be avoided whenever possible, but this meant that an atmosphere of medicalisation often attended the business of being on the road.

It all added up to a general feeling that my voice wasn't reliable. That in the context of individual concerts, if there were sound problems, I might not be audible enough. And then my voice might start to give out towards the end of the show. And then I might get a cold, which would threaten everything. Given that most singers begin a performance with a certain degree of nerves, even just the normal adrenaline rush of walking onto a stage, which causes the voice to tighten, the throat to constrict, it is usually only as the show goes on that you begin to relax, and the voice settles into its full strength. I would start out with that constriction, then maybe reach a point of relaxation midway through the gig, which I would just have time to enjoy before I'd start to worry about lasting through to the end.

What I'm saying is that stage fright is sometimes an entirely practical response to a set of real problems. It's not just about the disconnect between audience perception – 'You're a wonderful singer, we love you!' – and self-perception – 'I'm aware of all my flaws!' – it can also be the result of being in possession of the knowledge that, despite what everyone is telling you, actually there *is* something to be afraid of. Barbra Streisand famously didn't sing live for twenty-seven years, after forgetting her words on stage in New York's Central Park in 1967. It was a huge concert, with an audience of 135,000 people, and she has said that suddenly forgetting some lyrics, and being unable to cover this up, left her with an inescapable terror that it would keep happening. 'I didn't perform again,' she said, 'until they discovered teleprompters.'

When children perform at a musical concert or in a school play, we reassure them with soothing words – no one is there to judge you, everyone in the audience is on your side and willing you to do your best, and even if you *do* make a mistake, no one will notice or mind, because they all love you. As an adult performer such reassurance is meaningless and seems patronising – yes, the audience may love you and be forgiving, but on the other hand they expect and deserve to be entertained, and for you to fulfil your professional responsibilities by putting on a good show.

So said the voice of reason inside my head. My initial stage fright may have been born out of basic insecurity, stepping up in front of an unknown crowd who might not like me, and not having the born performer's ego or cast-iron self-belief. But my later stage fright was more mechanical in origin; less to do with my faith in the value of what I was doing, and more about my worry that I just might not get through it. It plagued me, and made me happy to retire, leaving behind the aspect of singing which brought me the most grief, but I have always been aware that my retreat from the stage contains a strong element of cowardice, and represents something of a defeat, a state of affairs of which I am not proud. In 2010 I decided to do something about it.

In the back of my mind I had long nursed the idea that one day I would try hypnotherapy. Like a committed smoker constantly deferring the decision to quit, I just stored this notion away, thinking of it as an easy Get Out of Jail Free card that I could use whenever I chose. 'I'll go and get hypnotised,' I thought, 'and chuck a few quid at the problem, and hey presto it will be sorted for me and I will be the new Fearless Tracey Thorn.'

It had been years since I'd sung live, and I'd come through the baby years when I was semi-retired from music, the children my refuge and my excuse, the reason why I could not be expected to perform on stage. I was back to recording now, and so it seemed like a good time to put this secret plan into action. I Googled 'hypnotherapist', chose one who looked as though she had all the right qualifications, made an appointment and soon found myself sitting in a tiny, stuffy consulting room, half wondering what I was doing, half waiting for the moment, any moment now, when I would be cured, hooray. The hypnotherapist was warm and friendly, and asked me a few questions about what the problem was and what I hoped to achieve. I dissembled a little, tried to make it sound simple and straightforward, when already it was occurring to me that it was anything but. This was years of trouble I was bringing into the room, and added to that was the fact that, being a natural sceptic and fairly resistant to all manner of alternative therapy, I was going against my whole nature.

I wasn't sure whether or not she knew who I was, but I explained to her that I'd been a singer for years and had always had problems with performing. I tried to package the problem up neatly, hoping the solution would be equally neat. I was asked to stand up in the middle of the room, close my eyes and visualise myself in a stressful situation. This in itself was stressful, but it didn't seem the right time to mention it, so I played along with the script we seemed to have set for ourselves and said that my stressful situation was being on stage in front of an audience. I concentrated on feeling stressed, trying to focus that stress on the imaginary stage rather than the real room. Meanwhile, she sidled up to me and, quite suddenly, gave me a nudge that knocked me off balance.

'Aha!' she said. The stress I was experiencing, through my imaginings, had unbalanced me, causing me to become ungrounded and unsteady.

'But you pushed me,' I said.

'Yes. I pushed you *very gently*. It shouldn't have been enough to knock you off balance. Now, I want you to pinch your thumb and index finger together, and think about feeling strong and relaxed while you do it.'

I pinched. I thought good thoughts about strength and relaxation.

'We're going to do some tapping. Tap here on your collarbones, and then on your cheeks, and your temples . . .'

I tapped. I pinched, and I tapped. I thought good, strong, positive thoughts.

Then I stood up and she came and nudged me again. I was ready for her this time, so I stood my ground, and apparently this was the correct thing to do as it proved that things had already changed. The pinching and the tapping and the good thoughts had already made me more balanced.

I'm too obedient for this, I reflected, too polite and non-confrontational. I don't like conflict, and I don't find it easy to disagree with people without getting stressed, and now didn't seem like a helpful moment to start challenging this concept. After all, I was here trying to help myself. Was this the time or the place to start playing the arch-cynic? No, I said to myself, shut up and learn something.

Finally came the part I had pinned all my hopes on, the actual 'hypnotising'. I'd always wondered – would I be the kind of person who would go under straight away and be barking like a dog within five minutes, or would I be resistant? I didn't want to be resistant. I wanted to be hypnotised, and made better, turned into someone who didn't have stage fright any more. I wanted someone else to take over my mind temporarily and cleanse it of the part that didn't work properly. I wanted to be cured.

She put on a CD of 'spa music', the least relaxing form

of music in the world. Noodly pan pipes, fretless bass. Treacly synth sweeps and occasional random harp. The music that has ruined every facial I've ever had, every massage, every seaweed wrap. Why, oh why, I always ask myself, can't they play a bit of Sinatra. Some gentle Velvet Underground tracks. The xx. Bobbie Gentry. There is a wide world of music out there that hath charms to soothe the savage breast, and still they play this shit, deliberately to drive you mad.

I gritted my teeth, sat back and closed my eyes.

'Imagine a truly relaxing, safe place,' she said, 'the place you always want to return to.' Mind a complete blank. Who has a stock image in their mind of a place they always want to return to? Do you? I don't know, the kitchen maybe – I could make a cup of tea, turn these fucking flutes off.

'Maybe a glorious sun-drenched beach, with the ocean lapping gently on the sand,' she said, clearly not immune to the persuasive powers of the holiday brochure.

'Yes, OK,' I said, 'that'll do. Let's have the beach.'

Tried to imagine myself there.

Uncomfortable in my chair. Could hear noises from the street outside; traffic, footsteps, voices. Tried to relax, to give myself up to it, but that felt wrong too, like I was faking it, like I was trying to feel hypnotised. Inside my head a little running commentary of sarcastic rejoinders, in a voice that I couldn't switch off.

The hypnotism ended. I was back in the room! I was booked in for a second session! And because I am, as I said, polite and non-confrontational, I went back for the agreed second session and went through it all again, and politely told her I felt better.

I am a model patient. Turns out I am a bit resistant, though.

I still haven't done a gig.

13

LITTLE MONSTERS

If stage fright is partly a fear of the audience, then it's worth remembering that from time to time there *is* something to be afraid of with audiences, and that when you move from the territory of having *listeners* into the realm of having *fans*, it is not always without its problems. At the beginning of my career I felt that the people who listened to my music and liked what they heard were like-minded people, my peer group, all of us equals. We had similar tastes in music, and knew where we were all coming from and what was important. I never thought of these people as fans, particularly, and though they often wrote me letters, I didn't think of these as fan letters. It's only when you become more successful that you start to feel yourself lifting away from the group of people who listen to you, and it's hard to tell whether that's just an inevitable fact of life, to do with your growing fame and success, or whether your audience has deliberately elevated you above them, and above yourself, by emphasising how much they look up to you.

I don't know whether it's possible to stop this happening; all I do know is that not everyone wants fans, and having them isn't always an entirely comfortable situation. I revere and admire many other singers and musicians, but it seems somehow undignified and maybe just downright weird to call myself a fan. 'I'm your biggest fan!' people might say, as though it's exactly what you want to hear, but quite often it isn't. I understand how, in the heat of the moment, bumping into someone you admire, it's the shorthand phrase that comes to mind, but the drawback is that it immediately sets up a relationship that is unequal, unreal, or plain unwelcome. I've been lucky in that I've never accumulated the kind of audience that bond to become a unique entity – like Lady Gaga's Little Monsters, the thought of which makes me shiver. But inevitably over the years there has been a handful of, shall we say, admirers, who have gone further than others in their devotion, and while they have been mostly charming, still it never fails to make me shy away, uncertain as to what it means to imply that someone who is, essentially, a stranger is so important to you.

An unusual, and striking representation of the singer-fan relationship can be found in Anne Tyler's novel, *A Slipping-Down Life*, written in 1969. It tells the story of a shy, awkward teenage girl, Evie Decker, who sees a local rock and roll singer play a concert, is transfixed by him and his performance, and begins to act out of character. She starts going to gigs, which she's never done before, changes her style of clothes, and stands front of stage to call his name out loud while she takes photographs of him. Her behaviour builds steadily to a bizarre climax when, in a moment of – what, possession? hysteria? – she cuts his name, Casey, into her forehead with a pair of nail scissors.

For its time this is an extraordinarily graphic representation of obsessive behaviour. As an assertive act of 'authenticity' it seems almost to prefigure the moment when Richey Edwards carved '4 Real' into his arm. Evie herself regards it as a kind of branding – she wants to mark herself with his name, turn herself into his chattel, imply a relationship between them, even if it's a distorted, and at this stage imaginary, master–slave relationship. To her it is an act of freedom, self-definition even: 'I believe this might be the best thing I've ever done . . . Something out of character. Definite. Not covered by insurance', even if from the outside it looks more like subservience and self-negation.

The singer, Drumstrings Casey, or Drum as he is known, exercises an almost demonic power over her. There is a hypnotic quality to his performance style – he sings, then in the middle of songs, goes off into unexpected spoken utterances, apparently disjointed nonsensical phrases, reminiscent of a stream-of-consciousness Dylan-esque performance. Because of this strangeness, Evie builds him up, both idealising, and in doing so, dehumanising him. When she sees he has a wristwatch on, she wonders, 'Did he wind his watch every morning, check its accuracy to try to be places on time like ordinary people?' So the singer can be a normal person! Who knew?

They become locked in a mutual dependency – his career never quite takes off and he starts to *need* her good opinion, regarding her as a sort of good luck charm, providing validation of his talent. Eventually she outgrows him, reaching the point where she denies that she cut the letters into her own forehead and insists that some other girl slashed his name on her face. With this denial she has robbed him of his crutch, and the book ends with him on stage, a lost and lonely figure, with no new songs to sing. It's a story of singer–fan dependency, and begs the question, who needs whom the most? Is it true warmth that flows from fan to singer, or just a kind of neediness, which can turn to dislike in an instant? When the two have a row Evie quickly renounces his talent – 'And your music is boring, it tends to get repetitious' – and equally, while Drum needs the support and love of an audience, he is often contemptuous towards Evie, who is, if you like, his über-audience. What exists between them is a toxic blend of need, fantasy, delusion and love, which turns to hate on the flip of a coin. It's why the obsessive fan can be scary, and is another reason why I would prefer to have an audience whose members regard themselves as admiring listeners – adults who are your equal, and who might respect what you do, but also respect your privacy, and your independence from them.

An even stranger singer–fan relationship is depicted in Arthur Phillips's *The Song Is You*. It begins in the usual one-sided way, but develops into something more complex, reciprocal and, frankly, disturbing. Middle-aged music fan Julian Donahue, reeling from the death of his child and the marriage break-up that ensued, hears a young Irish singer,

Cait O'Dwyer, who is a rising star. He becomes obsessed with her voice and her songs, finding meaning in them which inspires him to grieve (something he's been unable to do), but he also forms a stalker-ish attachment to Cait herself, believing that he has a unique understanding of her, and offers her artistic and career advice.

But the novel takes a curious path in which the obsessive fascination felt by Julian for Cait is both welcomed and ultimately reciprocated by her. Early on he scrawls a set of instructions for her on some coasters at a bar. They are irritating, slightly patronising and glib comments along the lines of 'Believe in yourself', 'Don't listen to anyone's advice', and even 'WEAR A BIT MORE MAKE-UP'. Mystifyingly, Cait finds these comments on her work to be insightful, and comes to feel that he understands her in a way no one else around her does. She even incorporates comments he has made into her new songs, so that they develop a collaborative creative partnership – the stalker's dream come true. None of this seems plausible to me, and as the relationship develops and becomes more entangled and bizarre, so it becomes even less believable.

They begin a long-distance semi-courtship, leaving messages for each other, dropping hints, teasing and never quite meeting. He follows her, taking off-guard pictures, trailing her through a park and recording her on his phone when she's singing along to her iPod. Instead of being freaked out by this, she is enchanted, and writes a song saying she has left a key under the mat for him. He goes to her flat where there is indeed a key under the mat, and once inside, he 'stood swaying in her living room, horrified for her that some maniac could do this too, and he wondered if he should somehow warn her'. Well, yes. Or perhaps he should get out of her apartment and stop stalking her. Like a maniac.

Julian's feelings about Cait are, fundamentally, generic fan-feelings about The Singer. In her apartment he feels that 'he had risen high, to an altar in the sky . . . and there he'd been granted a glimpse into the mysterious cult of a unique goddess'. Cait is a cypher; a figment of his imagination. But what's never quite clear is whether or not Phillips is satirising Julian's behaviour, or taking their mutual attraction seriously.

Both these books imply that there is a codependent quality to the link between performer and fan, and maybe there is some truth in this. We may all draw the line in a different place in terms of how close we'd like fans to get, or how keen we want them to be, and at its worst, the singer–fan bond can be a scary thing. Nonetheless, it is a fact that in order to sustain a career as a singer you need an audience to be more than just semi-involved, semi-interested. You need to draw them in, make them want to buy those records and come to those gigs, and however ambivalent your feelings about their devotion, it is the lifeblood of any long career.

14

MY LITTLE KINDRED SPIRIT

I finished *Bedsit Disco Queen* by remarking that I felt a bit like Lady Sovereign's mum, and quite liked the feeling. But really, if I feel like anyone's musical mum today, it's Romy Madley Croft's of The xx. Like me, she started singing and playing guitar while still in her teens, forming the band with her schoolmate Oliver Sim, to be joined by Jamie Smith a little later. Ben and I learned a few years ago that they were fans of ours and considered EBTG a prime influence, and at their request we recorded a cover version of the song 'Night Time' from their first album. I met Romy for the first time when she came to one of my book events, at The Old Queen's Head in Islington. We said hello afterwards, then sat and chatted, and got on like a house on fire, and someone took a photo of us. When I got home and showed the photo to my kids, they said, 'Mum, she looks more like you than we do.'

And it's true: aside from any spiritual or musical con-nectedness, we *look* like mother and daughter. We have the same haircut, the same pale skin, the same-shaped pointy chin, and faces which, when we smile, form a slightly embarrassed or apologetic expression. On stage we stare at our shoes, off stage we stare up at you from under our fringes. When we talk to each other I can hear that we both lisp a tiny bit, and have a similar speech pattern, hesi-tating lest we interrupt each other or tread on each other's sentences. We're polite, reticent, innately shy, and yet have both found ourselves inhabiting this least introvert-friendly of professions.

Born in 1989, she is twenty-seven years younger than me, wasn't even alive when I formed the Marine Girls, met Ben, recorded *A Distant Shore*, or the first four EBTG albums. She was only a child, sitting in the back seat of a car, when she heard 'Missing' on the radio and fell for my voice, years before she would suspect that she would ever try singing herself, or that when she did she would end up sounding a bit like that voice of mine on the radio.

Now, years later, she's more famous than me, and here we are in the Buzzin' Fly office in Clerkenwell talking about singing. I'll ask her the important questions first.

Me: Have you ever done karaoke?

Romy: Only once, when I was really drunk ... I sang Fleetwood Mac's 'Dreams'.

Me: I've only done it once, drunk, too. Mine was Will Young's 'Leave Right Now'.

She's already told me that, as a youngster, not only did she not dream of being a singer, or imagine being a singer, but was in fact so reluctant to sing, or to be heard singing, that she would mime when people sang 'Happy Birthday'. That's hardcore shy, I think, *miming* to 'Happy Birthday'. But this chimes with something I believe about the apparent contradictions in the stories of those who gravitate, sometimes reluctantly, towards singing as a career: there is a type of singer, perhaps a minority but nonetheless a significant number, who sings almost against their will, and despite an instinctive aversion to all forms of public display. These kinds of people sing because they need to more than want to, because it offers an outlet for bottled-up feelings they sometimes don't even know they have, and in singing, they present an alternative model to the audience, a kind of anti-singer, or at least anti-performer, which is the antithesis of showbiz and showing off. Romy tells me that she never knew she wanted to sing until she found she was a singer, had never suspected there was this person hidden inside her. And yet even now, when it has become her outward, famous persona, still she harbours doubts as to whether this unexpected turn of events is real, whether this is really her. Supporting Florence and the Machine, she talks about watching super-confident Florence on stage, a flamboyant born-to-be-performer. 'And me and Oliver would be thinking, who are we? What are we doing here? Do we even belong here? ... I felt a world away.' I imagine Florence-style performers, what we might call typical larger-than-life characters, *feel* like performers on stage, and that this is entirely natural. Romy, like me, says, 'I've always felt like a *normal* person on stage.' But do 'normal' people belong on a stage?

'But surely,' I say, 'audiences like seeing people like us on stage; they wouldn't come to see us otherwise. So maybe it's that in seeing us up there, they are seeing themselves reflected and represented, the normal people, having a go, being given a chance.'

Like me, Romy has been given pep talks about performance, about trying to extend her range, smile more, or not sound so sad. 'But how,' she wonders, 'how do I make myself sound not sad?'

'You really, really shouldn't,' is my only advice, and I'm reminded of that old line from our bass player Steve Pearce, who said to me years ago, 'You don't go to Frank Sinatra for the disco numbers, do you?' In other words, your identity is crucial, and for those who like you, it's what they like you for. If Romy and I both sound sad, because of something in the tone of our voices, or our range, or our tendency to fall off a note at the end of a line, and leave it hanging forlornly in the air, well, so be it, that's who we are. Though it wasn't inevitable from the start that she'd sound the way she does: that voice of hers, which sounds so natural and effortless, had to be found and decided upon. As a teenager her first attempts at singing were inspired by The Distillers' singer Brody Dalle (if you haven't heard her, she sounds more like Courtney Love than anyone else), but as a fourteen-year-old girl, she was unable to achieve that kind of gravelly, husky voice, and so gave up trying after a few days. Then came a period when, again like me, she began singing quietly at home, deliberately not projecting her voice, trying not to be overheard. 'I would stay up after my dad had gone to sleep, and barely whisper.'

*

ME: And now, now that you have to go on stage and be overheard by the crowd, what do you do before you go on, to prepare yourself, get your voice ready?

ROMY: No, nothing, it's quite a comedy actually, our backstage – there's all of us sitting really quietly, Oliver with his headphones on till the last minute. We get up, have a hug, and go on stage ... I play guitar a little bit before going on, but I never sing, and it's to do with shyness. I couldn't sing in that room ... even going to the toilet, if I sang in the toilet, if someone came in, I'd panic ... '

ME: So it's less scary to go on stage and sing for 6,000 people than to be in the toilet, where one person might come in and accidentally overhear you?

ROMY: Hahaha, yeah.

ME: That's brilliant, and I completely understand, but to anyone who's not a singer, it might sound a bit, um, mad.

ROMY: Well, when I'm on stage I think, yeah, I'm here, I'm *supposed* to be doing this, I'm here to do this.

So it's about context: where singing 'fits', or has its place, or is acceptable, or expected. If it's overheard outside of that context, there's an awkwardness, a feeling of something being stolen from you, almost, or intruded upon. We both agree that we hate the idea of anyone hearing us in the process of writing a new song; at home, Romy asks her girlfriend Hannah to stay the other side of a closed door and with headphones on while she is trying out new musical ideas, horrified by the thought of being eavesdropped on, even by the person she lives with. Is there safety in numbers, then? Does the crowd disappear a bit; can you make the audience fade out if you need to?

ROMY: Yeah, if you're playing to thirty people in a small room, I find that really hard. When you can see them face on, and you know who they are – like when we started, in a pub, where they're all your friends.

ME: Yeah, that's harder.

ROMY: In a bigger crowd, when it's dark, you can always zone out a bit. But then there's always someone who yawns in the front row, and you're thinking, oh God, is this really boring? It really breaks the spell.

ME: They've been brought along by their girlfriend, they're not the one who bought the tickets. What about speaking as opposed to singing, is that easier? Do you speak much on stage?

ROMY: No, I've tried to teach myself to speak a bit, to speak slower, to sound calm. But speaking's harder than singing.

ME: I find it difficult, because talking breaks the spell. When you're singing you're creating an image, then when you speak you dispel that image, and you have to recreate it with each new song . . . When Ben and I used to do small acoustic gigs, just the two of us, it worked better, just chatting to the audience. But at bigger gigs, if it's more of a production, and you're putting on more of a show, it breaks into that, to tell an anecdote about how you wrote a song. It feels a bit prosaic, when what you're creating in the songs is more poetic – like you're bringing everyone down to earth with a bump. Explaining how you wrote a song, or what it's about, it reminds me a bit of that Robert Frost quote, when he was asked to explain what a poem meant and he said, 'What d'you want me to do? Say it again in worser English?'

Of course, the big difference between me and Romy is that she does it and I don't. Maybe she's taken over from me, and I'm happy with that thought. She's inherited my stage fright but, like me, she's found ways of coping with it, strategies for getting through and carrying on. Touring makes the live experience become a habit, and that eases the nerves, but it can also blur the senses a little so that mistakes creep in. The xx play at a lot of festivals during the summer, which means weekend gigs with a week off in between, and during that week you can forget how to do it.

ROMY: I walk on and I'm thinking, what am I doing? Recently, I was doing that, and I completely forgot the song, just couldn't find the chord on the guitar, just kept playing the wrong chord. In the end I had to say, 'I'm so sorry, I can't remember this', and we had to go on and do another song. Oliver was laughing into the mic, and the audience were fine with it.

ME: Audiences are always fine with it; they like mistakes, the moments that make you human. But it's so hard to believe that when you're the one up on the stage. Do you forget words ever?

ROMY: Yeah, I do – I'll find I'm thinking, what's the next word? What's the next word? And if I don't think about it, it just comes out. I've even found myself, before a gig, Googling my own lyrics, ridiculous. I had to do it before Bestival, in 2011, the last European show of a tour, and I had to Google the lyrics to our first single. And I had to do the same thing on the last show of this tour – like I'd hit a wall or something.

ME: And that's funny, cos you'd think, the more times you sang it . . . but it becomes so automatic, you can't access it with your conscious mind. But it's weird the way your subconscious mind can do it – I've had that, where I'm getting to the end of a line and I'm thinking, I don't know what the next line is, I don't know what the next line is, and then it comes out of my mouth – and I'm thinking, I didn't know what the line was so how did my voice sing it?

*

It's good talking to another singer, who understands all this stuff. We've stood in the same place, wearing similar shoes, and looked out at the same view, with very similar thoughts in our head. I need to ask her one last important question, to see if we're really in tune with each other.

ME: What d'you think about *The X Factor*, d'you really, really hate it?

ROMY: Hahaha, no, I love it. My girlfriend Hannah said, 'Oh, look, Tracey's tweeting about *The X Factor* again' – this was before we'd ever met, and I thought, this is brilliant, seeing all of the things you said . . . I find it fascinating . . . I was going to say in my speech at the AIM Awards that if Oliver and I were on *The X Factor* we'd never have got past the auditions.

ME: Yeah, I watch with my kids, and they say, 'Mum, if you went on would you get through? Would you win?' And I say no, I can't do that, what they're doing! I can't sing that Whitney Houston song they all have to sing.

ROMY: Sometimes, there's like the token mousey girl, and you're thinking, I don't know if you're gonna win, you're just there for them to try and show a bit of diversity – and then there are the ones who do all that crazy singing that I would just have no idea how to do, so I feel . . . I don't feel like a singer when I watch it.

ME: It always reminds me that there are a lot of people out there who can sing, it's not *that* unique a talent. And sometimes, when people are going on at you – oh, you're such a great singer, you should be so proud of yourself – you can get a bit puffed up about it, and then watching *The X Factor*, it reminds you that a lot of people can sing.

ROMY: And a lot of people can sing better than me.

ME: That's what I feel too.

15

CUT TO THE CHASE

In my conversation with Romy we touched on the difference between singing and speaking and how tricky it can be on stage to go from one to the other. It made me think how strange it is that these two activities, which in some ways are so similar, actually feel so utterly unalike. On the one hand they are physically distinct, in that something different happens within your throat when you sing as opposed to when you speak. If you put your hand on the front of your neck and speak a phrase, then sing it, you can probably feel your larynx change position for the two activities. In modern classical singing, the larynx is lowered, increasing the length of the vocal tract, and this increases the resonance of the voice and gives it a darker, richer sound – but a sound which is distinct from the normal speaking voice, which usually employs the larynx held in a higher position, as does most pop singing.

But singing and speaking are mentally as well as physically distinct, and research has shown that the two activities use separate areas of the brain. In his book *Musicophilia*, Oliver Sacks tells stories of patients suffering from aphasia following a stroke, or due to dementia, who have lost the power of speech, yet are still able to sing song lyrics. This is possible only because within the brain there is a 'speech area' in the left frontal lobe, and if a particular part of this is damaged, then spoken language can be lost, while musicality, coming from the right hemisphere of the brain, remains untouched. Sacks writes that: 'Whenever I see patients with expressive aphasia, I sing "Happy Birthday" to them. Virtually all of them ... start to join in ...' Music therapy can often be beneficial in restoring at least some speech to such patients, beginning with the singing of phrases and moving towards a renewed ability to speak them.

However, even knowing about these separate areas of the brain, it remains mysterious and perplexing to us to think that a simple matter of adding a tune to words can so fundamentally affect our ability to voice them. In the most common speech disorder – stuttering – it has long been observed that even those with the worst stutter nearly always have the ability to sing without inhibition or interruption, and again, by singing phrases, or speaking them in a sing-song manner, they can learn to overcome the stuttering.

The gap between singing and speaking is out of our conscious reach, then; we cannot exert much control over it. In order to sing a phrase, we do something different to when we speak it, but we do it unconsciously. Speech is rarely delivered in a monotone, it is inflected, but when we start to sing we exaggerate the inflection and make it clearly and obviously melodic. We alter our breathing, too, particularly if we have been taught how to sing, and try to project the voice on an out-breath, which comes from as low down as possible. We try not to constrict the voice in the throat but to be aware of using the lungs, even the diaphragm, controlling the breath being the best way to control the strength and quality of the note. And quite often when we are singing as opposed to speaking, we use vibrato in the voice. We take vibrato for granted nowadays, particularly in classical, or 'proper' forms of singing, but this wasn't always the case. The use of vibrato wasn't considered an essential part of singing in the sixteenth and seventeenth centuries, but by the mid-nineteenth century it had become both more widely used, and somewhat controversial. John Potter mentions in *Vocal Authority* how Mozart was found complaining in a letter of the singer Meissner, who 'has a bad habit in that he often intentionally vibrates his voice . . . and that I cannot tolerate in him. It is indeed truly detestable, it is singing entirely contrary to nature.' Wagner, who was a singer himself, was a proponent of the idea that singers should sing it straight. 'The singers need only sing the notes,' he wrote, believing that the meaning and emotion were all contained therein, and did not need extra embellishment. It seems that lots of critics had a similar objection throughout the nineteenth century: John Potter also mentions how later, George Bernard Shaw complained that vibrato was 'sweeping through Europe like the influenza'.

This idea that vibrato is an affectation of the natural singing voice does not go away. Potter describes experiments carried out during the 1920s and 1930s at the University of Iowa in which recordings were made of singers' voices, in order to analyse them, by means of listening to slowed-down versions of the recordings. This way the presence and extent of their vibrato could clearly be heard and measured. The trained singers were found to use vibrato almost all the time when singing, while untrained voices rarely possessed it naturally. Other research tried to establish whether people used vibrato in speaking, and in normal speech it was found not to be the case, only appearing when a speaker was emotionally roused in some way. This was especially true in the case of actors. So, there is a sense in which we inevitably associate vibrato in the voice with emotion, or passion, and that is why it has now become commonplace in singing. It is shorthand for feeling. An add-on to the plain voice of speech, which flags up the emotional content of the sound that is produced.

It makes singing more patently stylised than speech, and for this reason has often been rejected by pop and rock singers, who fear its implicit lack of authenticity or naturalness and ascribe an almost moral failing to it. In an interview for Donna Soto-Morettini's book *Popular Singing*, Paul McCartney says: 'My tribe don't like vibrato – we think it's a fake, to cover up like it is in string playing, because you don't know exactly where the note is, so you 'vib' either side of it … Notice that the Beatles didn't do much of it. We used pretty much good straight notes, because there's something honest about it.' The pure sound of a real, honest voice is one with no vibrato – it's a widely held belief, shared by Mozart and McCartney, and clearly one that isn't going to go away. Like most rules, though, it's made to be broken. I can't think of a singer who uses more vibrato than Judy Garland; her voice throbs with it, every note pulsating, her body tense and alert like a startled hare. Yet she is the most movingly sincere singer, and far from sounding like she is trying to cover something up, she gives the impression of hiding *nothing*, leaving herself wide open at the end of every song; exposed, exhausted.

The dislike of vibrato seems connected to a yearning for some of the quality of speech to remain present in singing. The music journalist David Hepworth once wrote in a blog piece that he likes singers who 'sing like they talk'. He tells a great anecdote about being at *The Word* magazine and taking a phone call from 'a Tony Bennett', who, it immediately became apparent from his speaking voice, was *the* Tony Bennett. 'The voice speaking to me was unmistakably the same one that had sung to us all those years. He could no more disguise it than fake his fingerprints.' Hepworth goes on to talk about singers who sound like they speak, citing examples such as Christine McVie, and Frank Sinatra, who 'slipped from speech to song without stopping to arrange himself into the posture of a singer'. He contrasts this naturalness with the irritating behaviour of those who 'don't seem to feel they're performing until they've put on what they clearly think is a singerly voice'.

Many of us share this belief, then, that singing is more true, more communicative, *speaks* to us more, when it is more like, well, speaking. Twentieth-century avant-garde composers, such as Arnold Schoenberg, have tried to formalise this idea, and create new ways of using the voice that, instead of taking it into the recognised sphere of singing, let it remain somehow connected to speech. In his 1912 work *Pierrot Lunaire*, Schoenberg came up with the idea of a kind of pitched speech, or *Sprechgesang*, setting out in his foreword to the piece rules for how it was to be performed, with a strict attention to rhythm. His description of the singing style is enormously esoteric, and I wonder how many actually understood it then or now. According to Potter's *Vocal Authority*, it was important, said Schoenberg, 'to emphasise fully the contrast between the sung note and the spoken note'; the singer, or 'reciter' must not 'fall into a sing-song form of speaking voice', must clearly differentiate between ordinary speech and a kind of musical speech, 'But, again, it must not be reminiscent of song.'

Well, that's as clear as mud to me – how about you?

Even Schoenberg was apparently not often happy with the resulting performances, and many people simply found it difficult to interpret exactly what his instructions meant. It seems possible that he just didn't understand singing and singers, didn't understand vibrato and how it worked.

Others have noted that it is the very *difference* between singing and speaking which is the point, which elevates singing and gives it some of its meaning. Lavinia Greenlaw writes in *The Importance of Music to Girls* that 'we reveal something of our nature when we sing, something that can be disguised in our speaking voice'. When Romy and I talked about that awkwardness of going from singing to speaking, we admitted that there can be something jarring about the transition, especially if, like me, you feel that your singing voice has a character not shared by your speaking voice. When singing, I can sound confident and in control, there is something mature about my voice, it's even been described as 'classy'. Well, my speaking voice isn't like that; it's more down to earth, chatty, a bit suburban and ordinary. And so something of the magic or mystery is lost. I felt this recently, watching Jessie Ware perform live – the contrast between her rich, sensuous singing voice and more raucous, humorous speaking was funny. It had a charm to it, definitely, and she is totally likeable on stage; but still, there was a sense of illusion being created, then destroyed by something more prosaic, and having to be recreated with each new song, which subtly undermined the coherence of the show. Audiences always think that they want you to talk to them, but it is a fine balance to strike, between being friendly and preserving the mood.

For the distinction between singing and speaking is fundamental; the singing voice reaches both depths and heights untouched by the speaking voice, and singing is more revelatory. If we recognise as much, then we don't need to make singing more like speaking in order for it to be true. Even singing that we regard as highly stylised and artificial – operatic singing, say – can contain as much veracity as the plainest plainsong. There's a passage in Julian Barnes's *Levels of Life* where he describes how, during his intense grief after the loss of his wife, he developed a love of opera. He'd never liked it before – 'Operas felt like deeply implausible and badly constructed plays, with characters yelling in one another's faces simultaneously.' But now, in his state of grief, 'it seemed quite natural for people to stand on stage and sing at one another, because song was a more primal means of communication than the spoken word – both higher and deeper'. At this point he realises that opera is not really about the plot, but that 'its main function is to deliver the characters as swiftly as possible to the point where they can sing of their deepest emotions. Opera cuts to the chase – as death does.'

And if singing is ultimately more revelatory than speaking, giving away things we might prefer to conceal, then it is no surprise that most of us would be happier to speak in public than to sing. Singing, even if we were to sing the same words we might speak, turns those words into a performance, draws attention both to the words and to the singer him or herself. I have not sung on stage since 2000, but in 2013 I found myself travelling around the country appearing at promotional book events where I sat on a stage in front of an interviewer and an audience, and it was much easier and less stressful than singing. I don't suffer anywhere near the same stage fright when sitting on stage reading and speaking as I would if I were performing. (Although that's not to say I don't suffer at all, and a combination of beta blockers and wine is usually required to get me through.) The fact that I can do it confirms this idea that there is a level of exposure involved in singing which is much less in the case of speaking, but it does rather give the lie to my claim that I don't like to be looked at. I find when I'm sitting on stage talking that I don't much mind being looked at. And I think this is because I'm just chatting, making the odd joke. I'm not expected, in other words, to give a performance as a pop star.

Although one night, in Hull, I almost did. Asked what was a favourite lyric I had written, I thought for a moment and replied, '"Protection" is a good one.' 'Sing it!' shouted a voice from the crowd. And for some reason, I thought, yes, I will. I paused, took a breath, and in that brief pause the interviewer asked the next question. I don't know what would have happened if I had stepped over that line from speaking to singing – probably nothing – but it certainly would have created at least a moment of unexpectedness, and a change of mood.

Speaking is a more grounded experience; the spoken word never takes flight the way that singing does, partly because song lyrics tend to be more like poetry, a different register of language that is tacitly acknowledged as being emotional in tone. Singing would elevate the performance to a higher emotional level, but with the attendant risk of falling, and the greater sense of danger is where the fear lies. It's where the thrill lies, too, for the listener and for the performer, both of whom might enjoy the element of risk. For most people the gap between speaking and singing probably also incorporates a sensation that when singing they are amateurs, and fear losing control over their voice and the sounds or words it might utter. It's enough to make any of us feel vulnerable. It shouldn't be the case for the trained or professional singer, yet still I'm not sure that the vulnerability and potential for loss of control ever quite goes away – hence the angst we keep coming across in so many great singers.

The lesser anxiety involved in speaking, however, must be a result of the fact that with the spoken word we usually stay within the realms of the real, the normal, the everyday. As soon as we sing we move into new worlds; more fantastical, otherworldly, numinous. This can be used to great effect in drama, like the moments in Dennis Potter's plays when characters break into song. Potter was a great believer that, however shallow or meaningless popular songs may be, the emotions they evoke and trigger are not. The songs become useful conduits for all the emotions that people cannot speak. In his great 1994 interview with Melvyn Bragg, Potter addressed this directly, talking about the use of songs and lip-synching in *Pennies from Heaven*: 'I wanted to write about – in a sense it sounds condescending, and I don't mean it quite this way – I wanted to write about the way popular culture is an inheritor of something else. You know, that cheap songs, so-called, actually do have something of the Psalms of David about them. They do say the world is other than it is. They do illuminate. This is why people say, "Listen, they're playing our song", or whatever. It's not because that particular song actually expressed the depth of the feelings that they felt when they met each other and heard it. It is that somehow it re-evokes and pours out of them yet again, but with a different coating of irony and self-knowledge. Those feelings come bubbling back. So I wanted to write about popular songs in a direct way.'

Wittgenstein wrote that, 'Whereof one cannot speak, thereof one must be silent', but as Ian Bostridge points out in his *A Singer's Notebook*, 'That we cannot speak about, as

Wittgenstein realised in his late philosophy, we do not pass over in silence, but endlessly mull over in art, religious doctrine and, perhaps above all, music.'

Songs, then, allow us to sing what we can't say.

16

SONG TO THE SIREN

If singing is more revealing than speech, it can also be more dangerous and transgressive, with the potential to bewitch and enslave the listener, and I want to look at how this idea has been frequently explored in literature. I'm always fascinated when I come across singers in novels or poems, intrigued by what different characters or scenes can reveal about the ways in which singing is regarded, and what it symbolises for us at different times and in different places.

Once upon a time, learning a little piano and a little singing was a commonplace accomplishment for a young lady, another way in which she could be gently decorative and entertaining at social events. In the novels of Jane Austen, there are occasions when the ladies sing, but the singing has a strict social function, it's not expressive singing. Mary Bennett in *Pride and Prejudice* sings and plays at Netherfield, but her singing is out of tune and embarrassing, just as she is always a disappointment; the plain, dreary sister, to whom nothing ever happens. Her inability to sing is in keeping with her other shortcomings, and her overall status of being unattractive and unmarriageable – the worst failing for a woman. This kind of singing was operating under social constraints; the requirement was for it to be suitable, feminine, undemanding. Not too emotional, certainly nothing to rouse or unsettle the listeners, and perhaps it was also necessary for the singing not to be *too* good.

In Charlotte Brontë's *Shirley*, for example, there is a brilliant scene that shows how dangerous singing could be if it were done too well. The eponymous Shirley sings for a small audience, a traditional love ballad that she performs with unexpected fervour and passion. The result is something transgressional which disquiets her audience: 'On leaving the instrument, she went to the fire, and sat down on a seat – semi-stool, semi-cushion: the ladies were round her – none of them spoke. The Misses Sympson and the Misses Nunnely looked upon her, as quiet poultry might look on an egret, an ibis, or any other strange fowl. What made her sing so? *They* never sang so. Was it proper to sing with such expression, with such originality – so unlike a school girl? Decidedly not: it was strange, it was unusual. What was *strange* must be *wrong*; what was *unusual* must be *improper*. Shirley was judged.'

Shirley gives too much of herself away, moves beyond the constraints and expectations of polite parlour singing and expresses herself, in a way that embarrasses and unsettles the other ladies. Her singing is regarded as being almost sexually explicit; it has moved so far beyond what is required or expected. From the response, you might imagine that she has done a full Jerry Lee Lewis at the piano, hitching one leg up onto the keyboard, letting rip with unrestrained passion; the effect she has on her listeners is like Elvis on the Ed Sullivan Show. When the rules are so narrow and the limits of propriety set so tightly, it is not difficult to break them, to cross the threshold of decency. And so the forceful, passionate singing of a love ballad sets her apart and brings down the judgement of her peers.

In *Daniel Deronda*, Gwendolen Harleth sings as much as any young lady was expected to but her singing is more ornamental than anything else: 'She had the rare advantage of looking almost prettier when she was singing than at other times'. Singing, playing piano, doing needlepoint, a little sketching – these were the time-passing achievements expected of women of a certain class; none would have been regarded as art, nor were they required to be practised with any high degree of skill or commitment. In fact, too much commitment or involvement would be unladylike, and a threat to the status quo. In *Daniel Deronda* this socially acceptable form of singing is challenged by the book's Serious Artist, the musician Herr Klesmer, who describes the belittling effect of Gwendolen's type of singing. It is puerile and fatuous, he asserts: 'There is a sort of self-satisfied folly about every phrase of such music; no cries of deep, mysterious passion – no conflict – no sense of the universal. It makes men small as they listen to it.'

But really this is the whole point of this kind of singing: to keep things and people in their place. And the fear of

singing going further than it should – as it does in *Shirley* –
reveals an awareness that singing can be dangerous. It has a
power, an allure, a connection with sex. The legend of the
sirens dramatises this notion fully, and introduces us to this
thought: that singing can corrupt, defile and destroy; that
it may have a negative impact on the listener, and may
come from some dark place in the world's psyche.

Are the *Odyssey*'s sirens literature's most famous singers?
Certainly the tale of the sailor-adventurer Odysseus – who
stopped his men's ears with wax and had them lash him to
the ship's mast so that he could hear the sirens' song but not
be lured to his death – endures, and is taken up over and
over again by other writers who seek to make something
new of it, or retell it, or explain it. In the original telling,
the sirens use their voices to mesmerise and murder. Their
singing is dangerous, even lethal, and eternally fascinating.
We long to know what they sounded like, what their song
was, which contained such demonic power. The story
evokes a host of terrors concerning female sexuality, the
ability of the femme fatale to seduce and destroy, and it
speaks of ambivalence about the beauty of women's song,
and the power it exerts over us. Joyce's *Ulysses*, the most
famous retelling and homage to the *Odyssey*, is full of music
and singing, and bases a whole passage on the story of the
sirens. (James Joyce was a good singer himself, even con-
sidering it as a career option at one point, and I longed to
find a recording of his voice so that I could devote a chapter to him. I would have called it 'James Joyce Had a Lovely
Voice', but sadly I couldn't find any evidence of what he
sounded like, only descriptions, full of adjectives.) In the

sirens episode Bloom is tempted by the barmaids, and also captivated by the singing of Simon Dedalus, Ben Dollard and Bob Cowley, whose yearning love ballads enthrall the whole bar: 'Through the hush of air a voice sang to them, low, not rain, not leaves in murmur, like no voice of strings of reeds or whatdoyoucallthem dulcimers, touching their still ears with words ... Good, good to hear: sorrow from them each seemed to from both depart ...' Bloom stays longer than he intends in the bar, seduced both by the barmaids and by the songs, but he escapes in the end.

Margaret Atwood retells the tale again in her poem 'Siren Song', which seeks to get to the heart of the mystery of what the sirens actually sing, what the source is of their power. It has one of the sirens speaking directly to the reader – or to some hapless sailor – inviting confidence, flattering, tempting. And in this version it turns out that the sirens' power is not to do with the beauty of their singing, but with the persuasive content of the lyrics. The siren reels in her victim by claiming that she is a helpless, trapped female in need of rescue, and only this particular 'unique' man can understand and save her. The song works – and as she admits, almost in tones of disappointment, 'it works every time' – because it plays on the weakness and vanity of the listener, on the willingness of a man to believe any woman who tells him he is special. The poem ends with a stark warning: 'Now you know. Don't listen.'

In his short story 'The Silence of the Sirens', Kafka posits the idea that Ulysses only thinks he hears the sirens' song and lives to tell the tale; that in fact they are silent in the face of him, and it is their silence that he cannot escape.

'Now the Sirens have a still more fatal weapon than their song, namely their silence. And though admittedly such a thing has never happened, still it is conceivable that someone might possibly have escaped from their singing; but from their silence certainly never.'

I read that story for the first time quite recently, while I was researching anything and everything to do with sirens, and it immediately made me think of that mysterious group of singers, mostly female, mostly folky and from the 1970s, who disappeared, or just stopped making music, and in doing so cast a spell over critics and audiences. The silence of the sirens. That line I quoted above, it suggests that not singing can take on its own significance; if the sirens' singing is one kind of power, their silence is another kind, one we don't even understand.

You must know who I mean when I evoke these women who seemed to disappear. Queen of them all was Vashti Bunyan, who recorded the fairy-fey *Just Another Diamond Day* in 1970, then fled in a horse-drawn caravan and remained quiet for thirty-five years, during which time the album became a cult classic and was raved about by journalists and new folkies like Devendra Banhart and Joanna Newsom. She finally returned and recorded a second album in 2005, having in the meantime passed into the realms of musical mythology.

Scottish singer Shelagh McDonald also recorded her first album in 1970, then a follow-up in 1971, before apparently vanishing in 1972. It later turned out that damage to her singing voice had led her to seek refuge with her parents in Edinburgh. In the early 1980s she moved on again, losing touch with friends and family, and took up an itinerant life. In 2004 her records were rereleased on CD and again, a new audience was fascinated and captivated by the legend of a woman who had suddenly and mysteriously disappeared, or rendered herself mute.

And then there's Anne Briggs, with her artless delivery, for the most part gentle and vibrato-free, which reminds me so much of Alison Statton from Young Marble Giants, and brings to my mind again that quote I referred to in *Bedsit Disco Queen* about Alison being someone who sings rather than a singer. Perhaps this was how Anne Briggs regarded herself, too, even back when she did sing. She recorded one album, *The Time Has Come* in 1971, tried a follow-up but was dissatisfied with it and so gave up on the whole business of recording and performing. *The Time Has Come* grew in reputation during the years of silence, coming to be regarded as a lost classic, with original copies selling for substantial sums. And, as Alexis Petridis wrote in a 2007 *Guardian* interview, 'in her absence, the mythology around her has grown so immense that one writer compared her, in all seriousness, to Robert Johnson'. She herself was quite happy in her silence, raising children, doing other jobs, possibly more content than she would have been on stage. Never a natural performer, she is quoted as saying, 'I didn't like being looked at, so I'd shut my eyes half the time, trying to shut it out.' My sympathies entirely. She herself wore her talent lightly, though contemporaries recognised her uniqueness. Bert Jansch said of her that she was 'a brilliant, very natural singer ... she would improvise like a jazz singer'. But she preferred travelling and busking to recording or performing in clubs; perhaps she simply couldn't find the place or the space within music in which to be the singer and the person she might have been. I read an interview in which she confessed to feeling guilty at not making more of her talent, and also that she often missed singing through the years, but as for all the romanticising about her, and her silence, and her retreat, she seems to take everything with the same pinch of salt. She's almost bemused by the fuss made over her, which makes me think – and perhaps this is true for some of these other 'lost' female singers, too – that singing was something she only needed in her life for a while. Maybe it didn't really offer everything she needed to feel fulfilled, and a whole career of it would have imposed rules and restrictions on her that she simply didn't want.

Two other folk singers from this era – Shirley Collins and Linda Thompson – also stopped singing, though for reasons that were out of their control: both were struck by a vocal disorder called dysphonia. If you research online what happened to these two women, you'll find that the condition is often referred to as 'hysterical dysphonia'. It is said that Shirley Collins, who had recorded influential folk albums throughout the 1960s and 1970s, was so traumatised when her husband Ashley Hutchings left her in 1978 that the shock resulted in the complete loss of her singing voice, and she has never recorded since. Similarly, it is frequently suggested that the folk-rock singing star Linda Thompson, who had recorded seminal albums like *I Want to See the Bright Lights Tonight* and *Shoot Out the Lights* with husband Richard Thompson, began to be afflicted during their break-up in 1982, and that is why she barely sang at all for the next twenty years.

At first I accepted these snippets of information as fact. They make good narratives, after all, full of personal drama, cruelty and extreme reaction, and I took them at face value. Then, after a while, and after I'd written down my version of what I'd read, the two stories began to worry me. The use of that word 'hysterical', wasn't that a bit dismissive? Even a bit reminiscent of Victorian doctors, with their tendency to label women's physical problems as neurotic in origin, harking back to ancient notions of 'the wandering womb'? In both cases the vocal problems were neatly ascribed to heartbreak; the literal silencing of an abandoned woman. Too neatly, I started to think. Perhaps there was something rather glib in the packaging up of these undoubtedly traumatic stories, and I realised I didn't want to fall into the trap of repeating them as gospel. The only way to get at the truth was to ask the person who'd actually experienced the condition, and so with this in mind I got in touch with Linda Thompson, as I'd been meaning to do for years.

We'd met once before, in the Foodhall at Selfridges. I was having a sandwich and a cup of tea when a lady who'd been sitting at a nearby table came over to me and said, 'Hello, aren't you Tracey Thorn?' Ashamed as I am to admit it, I think I replied somewhat wearily, 'Yes, I am,' expecting to sign an autograph, at which point she stuck out her hand and announced, 'Lovely to meet you. I'm Linda Thompson.'

Now, this stopped me in my tracks, as I had only the

evening before watched a TV documentary featuring an old performance by Richard and Linda Thompson. She had been singing something glorious like 'A Heart Needs a Home' or 'Withered and Died', and I'd been struck once again both by her chiselled beauty and by the plangent, weary resilience of that lovely, unadorned voice. And now here she was, standing at my table, and I hadn't even recognised her. The coincidence of her presence, on top of my mortification, rendered me speechless, and I managed only a spluttering apology, followed by a gauche Bill-and-Ted-style 'I am not worthy', before we hugged and exchanged phone numbers and promised to meet up.

Due, I suspect, to mutual reserve and vagueness, it took a few years for this to happen, but finally I find myself sitting in her third-floor flat, looking out at the communal garden in all its spring glory, with the chance to get to the heart of her story, bypassing the internet rumours and finding out what really lay behind her retreat from singing.

'If you Google you,' I say to her, 'or Google dysphonia, you get this rather tidily packaged version of your story, and I didn't want to repeat it without running it past you first.'

'Yes, it is very glib,' she replies. 'Linda Ronstadt was the first one who said to me, Don't listen to the doctors when they tell you it's all psychological. And now, NOW they have found out that it is akin to Parkinson's. So now, after all these years, I'm seeing a neurologist, and having MRI scans.'

Which quite quickly puts paid to the idea that it is a 'hysterical' condition.

'Yes, although it does get worse with stress. And also

pregnancy. It was always worse when I was pregnant, and I was pregnant a lot of the time.'

I tell her that I read online about Shirley Collins being afflicted with dysphonia when her husband left her. Can it be that simple, I ask her?

'No, it's not that simple. And the same story is told about me, really – that I got dysphonia when me and Richard split up. But actually I got it about three months after we got married.'

So there you have it. Bang goes the theory. Ignore what you have read on Wikipedia. As I suspected, these stories are too neat to be true.

'I'm so glad I asked you,' I tell her. 'I didn't want to repeat these stories which seem to say, Oh, poor heart-broken women, their men leave them and they can't sing.'

'I know, it's so fucking annoying. There's definitely a psychological factor, but if something's part physical and part psychological and goes on for forty years, it becomes completely entrenched.'

And it affects your speaking, too, not just singing? (I can hear, talking to her, that there's a slight hoarse, croaky quality to her voice, a bit like someone recovering from laryngitis, and brief moments when there is a gap in her speech.)

'Yes. If I ask for a bacon butty and they bring me a cheese and pickle sandwich I sometimes can't say, No, this is the wrong thing. It's strange. It hits me at odd moments. Someone will say, Do you want this lipstick or that lipstick, and I go –' and here she mimes being completely mute, unable to get a word out, even to stutter.

I can only imagine the frustration of this. Later she tells me that it means she often avoids conversation, retreating from speech as much as from singing. I ask her how much of a loss it has been, especially the end of her performing career.

'Well,' she says, 'I didn't particularly love touring, but what I would love is to be able to jump up and join in with my kids when they're performing, get up and sing a chorus. But I can't, I just can't.'

Is that because you wouldn't trust your voice to be reliable?

'Yes.'

So it might work?

'It might, yes. Or it might not. If I sing in falsetto, I don't get any throat problems.'

But then you don't really sound like you.

'Absolutely right. But then I keep hearing singers of my age, you know, over sixty, and they don't sound like themselves anyway, cos the voice does go a bit, hahaha.'

She's got a gorgeous, smoker's laugh. I forget to ask her if she does or has ever smoked. Surely not, I think, but you can't always be certain with singers. It occurs to me, though, that she has told me her dysphonia started a lot earlier than people believe it did, and so she must have had long periods of working through it, recording and touring? It wasn't just a sudden, abrupt silence, an end to her singing, it was an ongoing struggle, something to overcome.

'I did, yeah, and it was awful, I never knew if anything would come out or not. And at gigs, the sound guy would say to me, I think you're going off mic all the time. I wasn't, but it was cutting in and out. I found out only recently that dysphonia is so specific, it usually starts at the age of twenty-six, which mine did, three months before I was twenty-six. Mind you, if I hadn't had dysphonia, I'd have never written a song. I was a singer, and that's what I did. But you have to do other things, when the singing becomes such a problem.'

I tell her about my stage fright, about the years of living with it, performing with it, and how no one who hasn't experienced it can really understand it, any more than they understand her dysphonia.

'People say to me, Oh, you'll be able to sing in *my* club cos it's very relaxing, but, you know, it's not *about* relaxing. I could drink a bottle of gin and take six valium, and I'd still have dysphonia. It's just a misfiring in my brain.'

Like me, she's had that feeling of the stage being a scary place, an arena of confrontation, and she says, 'In many ways, it's a sign of emotional stability, not wanting to put yourself in that situation. And when people say, I only really feel at home on stage, I think – I don't feel at home *at home*, never mind on stage!'

We laugh our heads off at this. They're just damaged people, I say, the ones who feel that, even though I'm a bit envious.

'Yes, I find them very annoying. A part of it's jealousy.'

As I did with Romy, we end up wondering how we ever ended up on stage, with that sensation that we didn't belong there.

'I always used to say to people I have the stage presence of a totem pole.'

A singing candle – that was Simon Cowell's phrase about someone on *The X Factor*. He said it very disparagingly one week and I thought, Oh, he's talking about me.

'I can't be doing all that "Oh, I love you guys", you know, or doing a lot of banter on stage, I just wanted to get the songs done. I've had that feeling, that I wasn't cut out for it – but then there are a lot of fans who would say, "But you *were*, I loved it".'

Yes, there are people in the audience who are sick of Entertainers, who want something different, more authentic, for want of a better word.

'Or in my audience,' she says, 'there'd be people thinking, "Will she get through it?"'

Which must have added a layer of excitement, I suppose. That unacknowledged desire of the audience to witness something dangerous, to see something that carries within it the risk of failure, of disaster even. And they're never aware of how much pressure even their happy anticipation can put on the singer. I say to her that we've both had the experience of people being a bit, shall we say, reverential about our voices, and that can make it harder. I've always worried that when I actually sing in front of people, they might think, Oh (disappointed voice), oh, she's not really all *that* . . .

'Yes, or that experience where you come off stage and people say, Oh, that was the best performance ever, when you think, it really wasn't . . . '

I ask her about the notorious *Shoot Out the Lights* tour of 1982, when she and Richard were over, bitterly over, but dragging themselves on, and she sang through a mix of pain and fury, apparently better than she'd ever sung before.

'I read recently that Richard had said to an interviewer, "Oh, that's rubbish – yeah, she sang well, but she'd sung well lots of other times before that." But in fact I felt it *was* really good, because I was broken-hearted, so I couldn't focus on this throat thing – plus I was living on vodka and antidepressants – so I could sing quite freely because something else had taken over. But it wasn't a very pleasant experience.'

Interesting, though, that at a time of such emotional distress her singing rallied. You'd imagine being sad would make any problem worse, but in fact one trouble distracted from another, and so reduced its impact. In the aftermath, however, she slipped into the shadows, recording only intermittently. In the last ten years, she has released three great albums, which isn't bad going by anybody's standards, but like me she hasn't really tried to return to the stage.

She says, 'There are people, aren't there, who just never stop. You look at someone like Bruce Forsyth – you know he's a hundred and ninety seven, and he's *on* all the time, isn't he? Always performing. Those kind of people, it's their life, their raison d'être, but it just isn't mine.'

No, not mine either.

'I feel now, in my dotage, that you just have to circumnavigate your weaknesses; you know, do something else.'

It seems that it is we the listeners who fret about the occasional silences of these sirens, more than the sirens themselves. Shunning the limelight can be seen as neurotic and unhealthy, but sometimes the desire to sing is simply not strong enough. The need to have a break from it all, to attempt a spell of 'normal' life, seems entirely comprehensible to me, but is often overdramatised by those who wish to pathologise privacy.

In their silence, or absence, these women acquired an aura of mystery and great significance. The work they produced before the silence came to be regarded with perhaps more solemnity and reverence than it really deserved. Anne Briggs, certainly, is fairly dismissive of her legendary album – there aren't 'any particularly good songs on it' – and the follow-up she tried to make she 'really didn't like' and refused to let the record company release. We want there to be something weird and wonderful in the reasoning that led them to retreat from a career we imagine as everyone's dream job. But so often, when we really dig into it, it turns out there is more of the prosaic and the mundane to be unearthed. The events that happen to all of us and interrupt our lives in one way or another. Illness. Heartbreak and divorce. Children. Or even just a sense that other people's dreams are not our own, that a ladder has been placed in front of us which we have no desire to climb, that there is something at the top we can't begin to imagine, or want, or need. But what does it mean, to stop singing like this? And can you even call yourself a singer, if you don't sing?

I asked myself this question occasionally during the years when I was not singing. That is, when I thought about it at all. I didn't disappear like Vashti Bunyan or Shelagh McDonald, but I had a break of seven years or so when I did no recording, and it is now fifteen years since I have sung live. We all have to fill in forms from time to time which require a job description, and I had always put 'Singer' – sometimes 'Singer/Songwriter', though I was never quite happy with that as it made me picture a little cartoon of myself holding an acoustic guitar – and I carried on doing so, even while I wasn't singing. It doesn't really matter, of course, what I call myself, but still, I wonder, is it a question of quality or quantity? In other words, can you only call yourself a singer if you're quite a good one, and get paid to do it? Can you only call yourself a singer if you do it regularly, sing live, go on tour? Or is it a role you assume at some point in your life, a costume you put on; once a singer, always a singer?

17

HEADS, SHOULDERS, KNEES AND TOES

During the years when I wasn't singing in public, I was still busy singing to and with my children. It was a revelation to me, how much singing was involved in childhood. Children sing all the time for the first few years of their lives, at playgroups and primary school – it's considered natural and normal, one of the first things they learn to do. Like painting, it's an automatic part of children's lives at this age, and they sing without inhibition or restraint. Frequently they have no sense of whether or not they 'can' sing, or whether the children around them can; it is more a question of who can sing the loudest, or remember all the words. Children are boisterous, ebullient creatures and singing can be a way of expressing or releasing some of that energy; it is joyful and unrepressed. There is an educational element, too, but not focused on the singing itself, more on the fact that singing can be a route to learning things off by heart. Somehow setting a list to a tune enables us to memorise it more readily, and so young children learn the 'A–B–C–D–E–F–G' song, and later some of them, my daughter among them, make a party piece out of learning Tom Lehrer's chemical elements song: 'There's antimony, arsenic, aluminum, selenium ...' For a while at primary school I had an extremely religious head teacher, who thought it would be valuable if we all learned to recite, or in this case *sing* the books of the Bible. And so I, arch-atheist that I am, can still sing for you the following: 'Genesis, Exodus, Leviticus and Numbers, Deuteronomy, Joshua, Judges, Ruth and Samuel, Samuel, Kings, Kings, Chronicles and Chronicles, Ezra, Nehemiah, Esther, Job, Psalms and Proverbs.'

So children sing for fun, and to learn things, and even at this very young age they sing to entertain. School concerts start early on, for the simple reason that nothing bonds a parent more fully to a school than the moment when you sit in the hall listening to a class of five-year-olds singing 'Away in a Manger'. In its innocence, simplicity and unabashed enthusiasm, the singing of young children is moving, reminding us of how we used to be, and of good things we too often overlook, or let slip by. Reminding us of the benefits of having a go, trying our best but not worrying too much, joining in. And so, trying to recapture some of this, we sing back to them, and with them. First, lullabies from the moment they are born, soothing murmurings of songs that we croon to them even through our boredom and exhaustion, the vibrations in our chest as we sing falling in with our heartbeat and adding to the comforting effect. I remember singing 'Dream a Little Dream of Me' to my smallest twin when she came out of an incubator, sitting in a rocking chair, feeling it as the first moment when she seemed more real, safer, with us to stay. I casually sang 'The Skye Boat Song' to the other twin one night, and was then condemned to sing it every night for the next year, after it became the only song that would help her drift off to sleep. And during the years when my children were small, this was the only singing I did. It was my period of retreat from the music business and from singing professionally or publicly, and so, having been in the limelight, I faded back into the crowd, realising that in this context singing had another meaning, and was not about how special you were, but about how much you could fit in.

When our children move beyond those first lullabies, we start going to playgroups with them, where it is expected that all parents will sit in a circle on the floor and sing 'Heads, Shoulders, Knees and Toes' no matter how problematic the tuning. The children themselves can't even speak at this stage, let alone sing, so we do it for them. Hand gestures are all that's expected of them, maybe a bit of standing up and bending down as dictated by the lyrics, but we, we poor unprepared parents, who have brought them here just to buy a little time, pass an hour of the day, it is expected that we will *sing*. No one ever really asks us if we want or feel able to, it just seems to be part of the job description of parent; yet another skill we didn't know we'd need and now have to acquire on the spot.

As for the children, well, they sing their way through

primary school, unselfconsciously, democratically, but as
they grow older they are often socialised into accepting and
adopting more formal approaches. By secondary school,
inclusive singing dwindles and it becomes a specialist subject, not part of the core curriculum. It begins to divide
along gender lines, too, so that from the age of around ten
or so there starts to be a split – girls sing, boys don't.
Singing starts to be considered a feminine activity. This is
the age when boys leave the choir and the girls learn
mawkish pop ballads from their singing teacher, like little
Jane Austen heroines, picking up a pretty parlour skill.
Ironically, at a different kind of school, or at a more 'serious' level of singing, this is the age when proper singing is
for boys, not girls, and only the pre-broken boy voice is
considered to have the requisite purity for serious choral
singing. Recent research has suggested this is an entirely
sexist tradition – that there is no rational basis for the belief
that boys have purer, clearer voices than girls. An experiment carried out by Professor David Howard, from the
University of York, consisted of a hundred and thirty
people listening to boys and girls singing the same piece of
music, to see if they could pick out the boys from the girls.
He said of the results, on the BBC website, 'If you have the
music the same, the rest of the choir the same, the director
of music the same, the acoustic the same, and you just
change the top line – you can't tell the difference.'
Interestingly, he also conducted further research to see
whether it was possible to define precisely what it was in
solo choristers' voices which made them stand out, and
indeed they found frequency peaks in the region up around

8,000 Hz, which create what he describes as 'this really shimmery sound'. There is an anatomical basis to this sound production, which is to do with how the larynx folds vibrate, but Professor Howard slightly ties himself in knots trying to elucidate precisely what is happening when we listen to this kind of singing: 'It's something that communicates with the soul,' he says. 'It's way beyond words, it's way beyond the music, it's something about the content going from the brain of a singer to the brain of a listener.'

So the old belief has been challenged, but is proving resistant to change. And meanwhile in schools and playgrounds, at a certain age, boys stop singing. At my son's school the music teacher cleverly circumvented this; noticing that all the boys were leaving the choir, she formed a boys' vocal group and got them to perform things like CeeLo Green's 'Forget You' and Snow Patrol's 'Chasing Cars'. At a school gala they took to the stage, a group of six of them, aged ten and eleven, and the girls in their year sat up like meerkats, noticing them for the first time as raw boy material that might yet, unbelievably, mature into something worthy of their attention. The group was considered a cool activity for the boys, and through it they were able to shake off some of the anti-singing prejudice that had accrued around boys in general.

Children who sing too well, though, stick out like a sore thumb and run all sorts of risks. We don't really know what to do with them, and the worst outcome is when we turn them into child stars. Pop music is an awkward place in which to grow up, and for those who start singing very young – like Michael Jackson – it can prove impossible to move from the rigidly controlled life of a prodigy into that of a fully functioning adult. Starting too young exposes you to the risk of stereotyping; you'll be given a label, 'cute', or 'virginal'. Charlotte Church, even though she started outside the pop world, was subjected first of all to idealisation, as a child with a voice of perfection and purity, and then later to demonisation as a wild child when she tried to carve out a space for herself as a normal young woman. Neither definition can be comfortable to live with, or come anywhere near the truth of what it feels like to grow up in public. TV talent shows, such as *Britain's Got Talent*, often introduce young singers whose voices surprise us – Lena Zavaroni types, barely out of childhood yet with the inappropriately lived-in voices of full-grown adults. This kind of unexpected talent can astonish and impress an audience, yet watching it always makes me uncomfortable, and I find myself asking all sorts of tricky questions – do these children even know what they're singing, have any understanding of the lyrics? Are they ready for the pressures and scrutiny of this environment? And is this even 'real' singing, or more like an imitation of it, a facsimile of emotions not yet experienced or understood?

To go from childhood singing – natural, unforced, communal – into adult singing – more complicated, personal, crafted – you have to pass through the teenage years, when your singing is more likely to be imitative and generic than perhaps at any other time. Glimpses of individual talent can shine through, but often these are the years of searching, of trying to find and settle on a voice of your own. I started singing in my late teens, old enough to have at least some idea of what I was letting myself in for, and emerged into a corner of the music business where individuality and character were prized above technical accomplishment or performance skills. I managed to swerve the packaged pop version of teen singing, that fast track to fame and fortune which can look so alluring but can actually constitute a mild form of child abuse, in which those too young to know any better are thrust into the spotlight. It's not the best time to embark on a career, or start defining yourself. Perhaps it's a rare example of a moment when the adage 'Children should be seen and not heard' is true, and it would be better if we didn't hear these kinds of child or adolescent singers. If only for their own sakes.

18

SUCH A LONG WAY DOWN

Growing up, I always wanted to impress my brother, who is ten years older than me. So I'd try not to be too much of a generic ten-year-old girl, with all the attendant girlish likes and dislikes, and instead focus on *his* likes and dislikes: learning to recite the names of the 1971 double-winning Arsenal team, for instance, or borrowing his Bowie and Faces albums to prove that I liked proper music and not the Bay City Rollers. But nothing impressed him as much as his recent discovery that as an adult I had once sung 'Who Knows Where the Time Goes?' on stage with Fairport Convention. I don't know where he was when this was happening, or why he didn't know about it at the time – often families are too busy to keep updating each other with their career progress, and so I suspect I simply didn't think to tell him, either beforehand or after the event. So it came as news to him when he read about it, years later, in *Bedsit Disco Queen*, and I felt that for once I had succeeded in impressing him, and then we bonded over a shared love of Sandy Denny.

He must have loved her before I did, of course. I don't remember hearing her records at the time they were released, and I first became aware of her when Ben and I listened to 'Autopsy' some time in the early 1980s. She's been there in the back of my mind ever since, as a voice with no real equal, and the more I have learned about her, the more she's joined my list of singers who seem to share and suffer from a similar array of doubts and anxieties as I do, and with whom I unerringly sympathise and identify.

She is frequently described as having 'the voice of an angel' – a description that exasperates and wearies me, and secretly I suspect she would also have rolled her eyes at it. Angelic is all wrong for lots of reasons. It makes her sound ethereal, transparent, unreal, or even just pretty and prim, and she was none of those things. There's an authority to her singing, an almost regal detachment. She is all dynamic range and power – almost as though her voice is plugged directly into a volume pedal. Even at her most gentle there is an extraordinary sense of control, so that her pitch and vibrato are sure and steady even when she's singing very softly – and then she can ramp up the volume quite suddenly and dramatically. Joni Mitchell has that command to her voice, too – listen to something like 'Don't Interrupt the Sorrow' and you hear a singer in charge of what she's singing. Dave Mattacks, ex-Fairport Convention, who drummed with EBTG for a while, always told me how loud Sandy sang on stage, and there's a story that she wasn't asked to join Pentangle when the group was formed by her then boyfriend Danny Thompson as her voice was just too big for them.

So, I imagine her, with this voice, this extraordinary voice, which we won't call angelic, but lacking many of the attributes of the natural on-stage performer. I have read descriptions of her being ungainly in performance, laughing off her fumbling with ad-libbed, self-deprecating jokes. It reminds me of Beth Orton, another singer who saves the seriousness for the songs and in between them is all clumsy clown. But everything I have read about Sandy suggests someone never quite certain as to where she, or her voice, fitted in. Veering between self-confidence and its sudden loss, drinking for fun and then not so much for fun, ambivalent about touring, and about success in general. And with a built-in sense of the inevitable descent waiting at the end of every high: in Clinton Heylin's biography *No More Sad Refrains* she is quoted as saying, 'I do appreciate being slightly well known, because I've got a bit of an ego. But I never want to reach the top. It's such a long way down.'

She was insecure about her appearance, and tried to cover this up with an air of bravado. Drinking and carousing with the lads, she was a ladette before the 1990s incarnation of such a thing was even defined. She paid her dues with the folk set, and learned any number of traditional ballads, but never had the purist's approach to the genre. A huge fan of Dusty Springfield, on *Fotheringay* she covered Dusty's early hit 'Silver Threads and Golden Needles', but she was equally drawn to ideas of singing jazz, or sounding like Janis Joplin. A diary entry from 1969, quoted in Heylin's biography, has her admitting to an experiment with a mixture of gin and Southern Comfort to discover whether it could help her emulate Joplin's vocal style. Heylin seems to find this difficult to understand – 'That the silver-tongued Sandy sought to replicate the "shattered effects" of Janis Joplin's vocals seems to beggar belief, but, in keeping with many aspects of herself, Sandy didn't want what she had – this 100% pure vocal tone – she wanted the stripped-raw rasp of a boozy blues singer.' I don't find it surprising at all. Many singers yearn for the voice they don't have, or strive to find ways in which they can stretch the voice they do have, push it further, break free of the expectations of others. It's not hard for me to imagine the constraints and irritations of being constantly told you have a '100% pure' voice. It's inhibiting and pat-ronising for any woman to be described as 'angelic'. When that is set against the boozy, raucous side to her personal-ity you have the makings of The Perfect Cliche, and it then seems obvious why she might wish to emulate someone rougher-sounding, who might be considered more soulful, more authentic, more real, less decorative.

Her ambivalence about success makes sense if we see suc-cess as representing not simply a larger audience, more love for her as a singer, but instead a different kind of audience, with different expectations and desires. She herself said that she suffered from a 'success neurosis', saying that as it got close, so it became more frightening – she liked the theory, but the reality scared her. I don't think this *is* neurotic. Surely as you draw close to something, you see it more

clearly, and what you might have perceived to be its qualities when viewed from a distance, or imagined or dreamed,
then prove not to be there, or to be distorted. A bigger,
more mainstream audience might, for instance, have had
views about the way she should look. In 1971 she did her
first solo concert at Queen Elizabeth Hall in London, and
by now there were high expectations placed upon her.
Used to performing on stage in jeans and a T-shirt, Heylin
recounts that on this occasion she opted for a long, floaty-
sleeved dress – only to find, in her nervousness, that it made
her trip over, knock over a glass, and then the long sleeves
got in the way of her guitar-playing. Leaving the stage, she
returned in jeans and a T-shirt to a standing ovation, but
still, the gig was far from an overwhelming success. She
knew that her ability to 'perform' or act the part on stage
could not live up to requirements as the stages and audiences got bigger, but what she seemed unable to do was to
find a way to fuse all the different aspects of her personality – the informal, humorous, lively character was at odds
with her more pained aspects, which she tried to hide, and
which only found an outlet in the elusive sadness of her
songs.

And growing success could mean a more 'pop' version of
success, which threatened her sense of authenticity and
belonging. We tend to think of folk singers as inhabiting a
separate musical environment, distant and sealed off from
the shallow ambitions of the pop marketplace, but there are
moments when the two worlds collide, and it's not necessarily a comfortable experience. I was astonished to learn
that in September 1972 Tony Blackburn made Sandy's song

'Listen, Listen' his single of the week, and it reminded me of the time in 1984 when our EBTG single 'Each and Every One' became a favourite of his, and of the awkwardness we felt at being catapulted out of our safe indie surroundings into the glare of pop radio. Sandy Denny apparently had similarly mixed feelings: not simply uncomplicated celebration of scoring single of the week, but also apprehension that it either would or wouldn't succeed. In fact, the single failed to be a hit, and when the album it was taken from flopped she began to worry that her moment had passed.

Along with anxiety about career success, she had to deal with the fact that many around her wanted her to pursue a career as a solo artist when she preferred the safety-in-numbers and the camaraderie of being in a band. Feeling that she wasn't cut out to be a solo performer but under pressure not to hide behind a band, she started to rely on drink to calm her nerves and then gave flawed performances which attracted criticism and as a consequence worsened her stage fright. This is how neurosis can take hold – experiencing reasonable fears and inhibitions, encountering practical problems that lack easy solutions, and then spiralling into uncontrollable fear.

Audiences, record companies and band members often wanted one thing from Sandy while she wanted another, and when a set of reviews criticised her arrangements, strings and brass, and suggested she should record more pared-down tracks, she performed a *BBC In Concert* completely solo, despite obviously feeling self-conscious about it. 'As you've probably noticed I haven't got my band with me tonight,' she said. 'I thought I'd try and do it on my own . . . I don't know much boogie-woogie, so you'll just have to put up with *this*.'

Self-deprecation can be endearing, of course, and it's really the only available stance for those of us too aware of flaws and failings to be able to tough it out, but imagining oneself in the audience at that gig, you can only wish it were possible to convey to a singer exactly how much they were loved and forgiven. But so often all they can see is, *I can't be everything to everyone, I can't possibly fulfil these expectations. This is all I have, and it's not much, is it? You'll just have to put up with* this. Oh, Sandy.

19

ME AND MY MICROPHONE

There's nothing quite like the bond between a singer and their microphone; it's symbolic, visually representative – hold up a hairbrush to your mouth and everyone will know you are 'singing' – and it's ritualistic: like holding a cigarette, it gives you something to do with your hands. Your relationship with the mic at a live gig is an intimate one. You can handle it, for a start, either gripping it and its stand, whole kit and caboodle, entering into a kind of dance or embrace with an object that is as tall as yourself, almost another body to cling onto; or you can unclip it and hold it in one hand, drawing it in close towards you, something small now, just a prop, a tool. Since the mic was invented singers have vied to come up with new ways to hold it and its stand. In his great book about the 1930s crooners, *You Call It Madness*, Lenny Kaye (writer and also Patti Smith's guitarist) describes Russ

Columbo's casually intimate stance: 'He holds one hand on the microphone stand, and puts the other in his pocket. It looks curiously as if he is dancing with himself, using the microphone as partner.' Young Sinatra famously clung to the mic stand, twining his skinny body around it as if for support, or as if he were clutching at a lover. Rod Stewart would take hold of the mic and kick the bottom of the stand up towards himself, catching it in mid-air, then holding onto it like a soldier with a pike, and Freddie Mercury adapted this move with his horrible little half-stand, that ugly truncated stick that managed to look both aggressive and weedy.

On stage, your mouth can actually make contact with the mic, your lips touching it. Every note you sing comes out on an exhaled breath, a sigh carrying tiny droplets of water, so as the evening progresses, the mic gets wet, and now your lips are brushing against moist metal. I remember that feeling, the closeness, just you and your mic, it's your best friend up there. And then, at the end of the evening, you leave behind physical evidence of your presence and your closeness; lipstick traces and DNA, you're all over that thing.

In the studio it's different – the microphone there has to be treated with more respect, it keeps its prim distance. Suspended in an elastic cradle at the top of a mic stand, it is not to be touched, and definitely not to be removed. It sits behind a nylon pop shield, whose purpose is to soften any over-emphatic consonants, and in the old, basic days, would be made of a leg from a pair of tights stretched over a bit of coat hanger. Later, in proper studios, it was replaced by an altogether neater, purpose-built gadget, made of black metal and black nylon. But still, the mic is at one remove from you; you're here and it's over there, your lips can't touch it, and the sensation you've got used to, of breathing words directly into its ear, you can't have that here. You have to sing politely towards it from behind an invisible line. It's a smouldering look rather than a full-on snog.

But what you've lost in oral intimacy you get back via the headphones. In the cocoon of the studio, with every sound separated and under complete control, you can have your voice as loud as you want it with no extra effort on your own part. On stage you use a near-field microphone, so that as far as possible it picks up only what's close to it – your voice – and less of what's further away – the drums, the audience. But in the studio, where you're the only thing making a sound, the mic will be wide open, ready and eager to receive the slightest sound that falls, the smallest whisper. It's like a magnet, attracting every little iron filing of your voice, sucking up sound from the atmosphere. Listen: before the track starts, in that silence before you begin, there's not even silence. You can hear every breath you take. Your lips part with a faint click, you can hear your tongue brush against your teeth. It's disconcerting at first, inhibiting even, but soon you come to love it. Imagine – if your breathing sounds that loud and close, how *huge* your voice is going to be. You can try *not* to make too much in the way of mouth-noise in between each line, but don't worry either way, it can all be edited out. And you can even go in the other direction, and use the microphone's attention to each sound to your advantage – make it hear and record every breath, amplify that breath, show them how hard you're working. I did this on the track 'Shoot Me Down', from the *Love Not Money* album. We took a sharp intake of breath, and ratcheted up the volume, using it at the beginning of the track before I start singing to create an atmosphere of tension and anxiety. As the track progresses, the vocal is heavily compressed, which again emphasises every in-breath, until by the end it's as though I'm gasping for air, half drowning in the pool of the song. Rufus Wainwright does this all the time – deliberately or not, I'm never sure. But you can certainly hear each breath, drawn in tightly through gritted teeth. Listen to a song like 'Dinner at Eight', and the drama of the in-breaths, every one as audible as the words he is singing. The effort is palpable, no false impression of ease here. Some have commented on this, criticising his breathing technique. Me, I like it, the way it adds a layer of repression to even his most expressive songs, the implication being, 'I am singing this *against my will*, that's how much it costs me.' Oh, what a little microphone can do.

How on earth did singers manage without them, before them? Although invented in the late nineteenth century, microphones weren't developed until the 1920s, and given that no electric instruments had been invented at that point, the microphone was the starting point for all that followed. Singers who pre-dated the microphone had of course to rely on their own vocal power for amplification, or made use of whatever they could find to give them an edge over the volume of the band. Rudy Vallée, for instance, became famous as The Man with the Megaphone, using a cut-down half-megaphone to reach an audience. Lenny Kaye talks about how certain singers responded differently to this new invention. Rudy Vallée embraced it, unlike certain other performers who were spooked by it and couldn't understand how this piece of machinery could possibly do their voices justice. 'Early on, Vallée recognised it as another instrument ... When he saw the effect his voice had on radio, he cobbled together one of the first in-concert amplification systems, complete with carbon microphone and several radio receivers. It was even more sensuous than the megaphone in its ability to reach out, to throw his voice like a ventriloquist so that it seemed to emanate from right next to the listener ...'

This was the key to the new invention, its ability to deliver the singing voice seemingly right into the ear of the listener, and it was a gift to the crooners, fostering their technique of vocal intimacy. Bing Crosby famously made good use of the microphone, as it suited his natural ease and expressiveness. He even adjusted his voice to suit the mic – he'd always made use of both his upper and lower ranges, but gradually, as Lenny Kaye put it, 'his baritone seems to expand in sonority, catching the resonance and warmth of the microphone's condenser'. Sinatra, too, understood the mic and, as Simon Frith mentions in *Performing Rites*, in later years said, 'Many singers never learned to use one ... They never understood, and still don't, that a microphone is their instrument.' He was a great believer in using the mic carefully, moving away and back in again as necessary, and deliberately avoiding any excessive breathing sounds. What he was aiming for was mastery and control; the opposite approach to Rufus Wainwright's drama and tension.

The introduction of the microphone, and the growing importance of radio, brought about a change in singing and in music in general. Previously, singing required power and volume, an extrovert approach that allowed communication with a large group of listeners. But now, singing could become more personal and draw the individual listener in close. It might sound obvious, then, to observe that the microphone allows for a 'truer' representation of singing, one which doesn't need to rely on sheer vocal volume in order to impress. And yet, for quite some time there were still those who distrusted the mic and perhaps saw in it the first example of studio trickery: a gadget which allowed charlatans to pull the wool over people's eyes – or ears, we should say. In *Vocal Authority*, John Potter describes a 1947 singing manual by George Baker, which has a chapter on 'The Voice and the Microphone': 'He does not consider stage performance at all, confining his remarks to broadcasting and recording except for a swipe at crooners, whom he describes as "fakers" and "vocal cheats", with the majority of them not having "voices, as such"'. It's as though the invention is doing too much of the work, and some of the human effort has been lost. The belief is that those who make use of this new invention, benefiting from it and exploiting its advantages, are in fact not 'proper' singers at all. There's definite suspicion and even disdain on the part of this listener. Comparing this with modern attitudes towards Auto-Tune, you realise that the distrust of technology which enhances or 'helps' the voice has been around for as long as the technology itself.

The new microphones affected performance in another way, too, in that they enhanced what the singer heard, just as much as what the audience heard. Instead of relying on your own instinct about how you sounded, and responding to the audience's mood and reaction, now you could clearly hear your voice out there in the room, amplified and enhanced. And hearing your own voice in this way, you cannot help but respond to the sound, and the volume – so that in fact you're not just singing to the audience, you are singing to yourself. Every singer knows the effect this has on you. Once music moved into the era of complete amplification, with singers singing into a microphone in front of amplified electric instruments, the issue of what the singer could or couldn't hear became paramount. Initially, pop and rock singers operated with monitors on stage – speakers shaped like a wedge of cheese, angled towards you, that provided you with a mix of your voice and the band, ideally set at a perfect balance, and loud and clear enough to be heard even over the sound being projected out in front to the audience. This is the ideal world scenario, though, and in the real world, in small sweaty clubs or in awkward large auditoriums, on-stage wedges, often so chewed up and knackered as to be worthless, failed to deliver anything to compete with the sound in the room, or worse still, the sound echoing back at you from the hard rear wall of the venue.

The invention of in-ear monitoring, which like most singers I began to use in the 1990s, changed all this. I had moulds made of the inside of each ear, which were cast into plastic hearing aids containing tiny speakers – a more sophisticated, personalised version of your iPod earphones. Attached to a power pack, which in turn had to be attached to your body somehow – awkward with certain outfits, since it required waistbands or belts to be clipped onto – the in-ear monitors would then remotely receive a mix of whatever you wanted to hear: maybe a blend of the whole band, or just your vocal and some piano or guitar to tune to, or – and this could be really tempting in certain circumstances – just your vocal. From barely being able to hear yourself on stage, the situation was transformed into a whole new scenario, in which you could hear yourself all too clearly. At first this seemed ideal, and the downside only became apparent later: that it was all too easy for the singer to be hermetically sealed off from the surrounding music, existing in a sort of bubble of vocal clarity, hearing something that no one else in the room was hearing – the voice in splendid isolation. In the technical sense this problem is usually one of tuning – hearing too much vocal at the expense of any instrument means that you can be singing in tune with yourself, but not with the rest of the band. Also, the clarity of the sound in your ears can make you reduce the projection of your singing, encouraging a singer like me to sing even more quietly than usual; great for saving the voice for the duration of a gig, not so good in terms of providing enough volume for the out-front sound engineer to work with. But perhaps even worse, it creates a performance problem, an attitude problem. Hearing yourself with this degree of fidelity, you can become overcareful, pernickety, singing more to impress yourself, or at least to avoid mistakes, than to communicate with the audience. Live performance should always have a sense of immediacy, of living for the moment, which comes from the belief that the sound you are making is essentially impermanent: it appears, is heard and then immediately lost. Your voice goes out there into the crowd, into the ether, and if you can't hear it too well it is much easier to immerse yourself in this idea of it being ephemeral, fleeting. For me, with in-ear monitors, live singing began to take on some of the quality of singing in the recording studio, with headphones on, your vocal way up loud, the balance just right. But this is a different kind of singing, this is singing on the record. Everything you sing is being taken down and might be used against you. It makes you feel that every word, every note, really matters, which weighs heavily. This might be a good thing, but it's the opposite of the abandon, the giving yourself up to the moment, that is the hallmark of the really great live experience.

It's ironic: I longed to be able to hear myself on stage, and then when I could I realised that it was a mixed blessing, that something chaotic and uncontrollable had been lost for ever. I had thought I wanted it all to be perfect, but when perfection became a possibility, it brought with it new demands and expectations, new things to fear, new ways to worry. Or perhaps that was just me.

As we've seen, this new era of amplification that dawned with the development of the microphone in the 1920s coincided with the story of the crooners, whose intimate style it facilitated; and I guess my interest in them is enhanced by the fact that I'm something of a crooner myself. Often regarded as sissy – the crooners' songs were seductive, aimed directly at women, and sympathetic to female dreams and desires – these men didn't perform the songs in any expansive or assertive way, they just stood there, calm, passive, murmuring their gentle sweet nothings.

Rudy Vallée defended himself against accusations of weediness: 'Most of the so-called crooners like myself are able to sing with considerable volume when the occasion demands it.' He also pointed out the skill that close mic'ed singing requires: 'The voice must be brought down to an extreme softness or pianissimo. This is quite an art, as most persons are unable to stay in pitch when singing extremely softly.' Still they were held in slight disdain, *Variety* saying of Russ Columbo that he was 'a freak radio singer, who is not a performer ... of the Bing Crosby flash-in-the-pan style of ether exhaler'. But this style of singing was no flash in the pan; it was here to stay. The introduction of the microphone and the growing importance of radio brought about a change in singing and in music, replacing volume and bombast with intimacy and ease.

Lennie Kaye points out that, after its initial heyday, crooning persisted through the decades, via singers like Billy Eckstine, Johnny Mathis and Chet Baker. Even Elvis, with what Lavinia Greenlaw describes as 'his mansion of a voice', inherited something from the crooners, and in some respects carried on where Sinatra left off – not least in acquiring, like Frank, hordes of screaming fans. You can trace the influence of crooning through Jim Morrison and Bryan Ferry; and in recent years I'd identify a strand of alternative-style rock bands with a croony male lead singer, as opposed to the rockist shouter of old. For a while, the yearning, mellifluous male vocal became almost the norm, by which I mean singers like Morrissey, Mark Eitzel, Richard Hawley, Stuart Staples, Paul Buchanan, Guy Garvey and Thom Yorke.

Bands with croony male lead singers will always sound perhaps more comforting than they'd like. While that may not be a problem for Elbow or Coldplay, who both seem content with their status as anthemic stadium balladeers, for a band like Radiohead you suspect that the innate loveliness of Thom Yorke's voice leads them to go to ever greater lengths to subvert it. As with Scott Walker, the constraints of the melancholy but beautiful croon start to become more apparent over time, so that careers which begin in beauty – 'High and Dry', 'Angels of Ashes' – start to fracture into a denial of that sumptuousness, an overwhelming need to shatter and break free of its imprisoning softness.

I made a comment on Twitter once about Guy Garvey being such a *reliable* singer, a safe pair of hands. Some people responded indignantly, implying that I was damning him with faint praise, but I hadn't meant it that way at all. I love the feeling, as soon as he starts to sing, that you can relax into his performance, you're released from any anxiety about whether he's going to carry it off. The certainty of his voice envelops you like a strong pair of arms; nothing bad can happen while Guy is singing.

Nonetheless, that in itself is a kind of limitation, and one

I probably share. To have a voice which soothes and comforts can be a wonderful thing – Lord knows we all need soothing and comforting – but does it rule out the possibility of danger? We don't want music to be an entirely risk-free activity; there needs to be some tension, some sense that the safety net is not guaranteed. Can such a voice also inflame and inspire? After all, no one wants to lull *all* the time; that would be soporific and numbing, a kind of vocal valium. Which is why the calming voice, more than any other, relies on context to give it deeper or alternative meanings, jagged edges, contrasts, unexpected juxtapositions. Some listeners didn't understand why Ben and I introduced more electronic elements into our music as we went along, but it was at least partly a search for new contexts for my voice, a way of making harder noises, with sharp edges, to offset my warmth and softness. A way of adding an irritant, a little bit of grit.

You know the way you're shocked by what you sound like when you hear your recorded speaking voice played back to you? People ask me if it's the same with singers – am I surprised by hearing my recorded voice? Of course I'm not any more, not after all this time. But what I am still shocked by is the discrepancy between the effort that goes in and the apparent ease that comes out. It's exasperating to me, this contrast. Singing that feels to me so difficult, so full of angst and emotion while I'm doing it, ends by sounding languid, calm, rational. When I sing in the studio you'd be surprised at the obvious effort I'm making: I screw my eyes up, and do funny things with my hands, and frown at the microphone, and lean in close to it, and back off for louder notes, and it all feels very active and slightly out of control. But the result is a sound that people say is easygoing, calming. I saw a great bit of footage recently of Marvin Gaye in the studio, recording a lead vocal, mic in his hand, *lying down on a sofa*! Now *that* is what I call easygoing. But Karen Carpenter, did she sweat and struggle? Did she long for more to be heard than just the softness, just the croon? Is it a mistake, all the effort not to let the effort show?

20

SPOOKED BY THE BEAUTY

It's hard not to make assumptions about Scott Walker: few careers have spanned so many years, and encompassed such dramatic stylistic changes. And, for those of us who adore some of his solo records, while finding his later work hard to listen to *in the extreme*, it's difficult to talk about his singing without sounding arrogant and presumptuous, without making claims that he might deny vehemently, and without straying into territory that may be pure fantasy and wishful thinking. But it has to be talked about, doesn't it? The simple fact that Scott Walker, possessor of one of the most gorgeous, luxuriant, enviable voices of all time, made a decision to put that particular voice of his away in a box somewhere; felt that he, or we, had simply had enough of it. It's not that his voice aged or worsened, was damaged by time or neglect, or any of the other things that happen to singers' voices over the years, and that he became *unable* to sing like that, it's that he *chose* to stop singing like that.

His performance on David Arnold's 'Only Myself to Blame' in 1999 shows his voice still intact, still lovely, but on his own recent records he has definitively left behind that overwhelming beauty. I can't help but wonder why, and sometimes think I know the answer, and sometimes – presumption above all others! – feel I might even understand and sympathise.

Did that voice of his get in the way? Was it a barrier to seriousness, or being taken seriously? Was it always going to confuse people to be coming on like Bertolt Brecht while sounding like Jack Jones? If you have a 'difficult' voice, you can sing easy songs. The kind of non-singers I wrote about earlier – they can sing covers of Burt Bacharach songs and make them sound edgy, get kudos for their reinventions of classics. As if they have cleverly dug deep and found previously unrecognised qualities within these simple tunes. If, on the other hand, you have a beautiful voice, it is not always so easy to make those songs sound fresh. Simon Frith writes in *Performing Rites* that 'the "difficult" appeals through the traces it carries of another world in which it would be "easy"'. In other words, it allows us a glimpse of an alternative mainstream culture, one perhaps with greater depths, or wider boundaries, in which more was possible and more was understood. Scott Walker is perhaps the greatest example of how far you may have to run to explore those depths and escape the confines of your beautiful voice. It's possible that he would have wanted to make his later records exactly as they are, whatever voice he had. But

I would argue that there is something about being in possession of that particular sound that drove him to go as far as he did.

The old Scott Walker voice was a smoothly delivered baritone, with elegantly slurred vowels and few rough edges. In an interview with Simon Hattenstone, Walker commented that 'People do feel a warmth with baritone voices that they don't feel with others. It's like the sound you get from a cello, and people love that sound straight away.' He was gifted with extraordinary breath control, making his singing sound effortless, with no hint ever of strain or stress, the long, held notes seeming to glide along on one intake of breath; certainly you never heard him take another. No high drama gasping from Scott Walker. His voice was always placed very up-front in the track, putting him solo in the spotlight, a completely un-rock-and-roll vocal placement. In other words, it was an MOR voice, but often singing non-MOR content. In the book *No Regrets: Writings on Scott Walker*, editor and contributor Rob Young says Walker had 'the loungey, laidback showmanship of Jack Jones and Frank Sinatra'; but even at his most MOR there was always more going on with him than was immediately apparent.

There's a deceptiveness about it all, an illusion of ease, as he lures you in, only to deliver the sucker punch of challenging content. Jarring lyrics within soothing arrangements, a juxtaposition that I've always liked. A sense of having it both ways; ease and its opposite all at once; pleasure and pain; the lovely and the not lovely. I can't think of another singer from the world of pop who sounds more like a grown-up than Scott, with all the richness and complexity that implies. In that, of course, he owes more to the world of pre-rock showbiz than to the other young men who were his contemporaries. He sings to you in that baritone, adult to adult. It's flattering, comfortable, such a *relief* to come home to. And yet, that voice doesn't truly relax or soothe me. In fact, it stirs me up a bit, sets off intangible yearnings and longings. It's the romanticism of the setting – all those searching strings – combined with the almost detached vulnerability he conveys. There's something lost about him. The songs often sound almost like dream sequences – sleepy, warm, but a little disconcerting. And in interviews now he talks about his voice with detachment, bemusement even; yet another revered singer who can't quite feel at one with their voice, can't quite understand it, or understand what all the fuss is about. 'It's a beast all on its own,' he said in the interview with Simon Hattenstone. 'I think of it as another thing, another person. When it's working well I couldn't wish for anything better. But it's temperamental. Sometimes you get up and he's just not ready to go.' In a 2006 interview quoted in *No Regrets*, he says, 'Singing is a great terror for me anyway, so it's something that I've never wholly looked forward to. When I'm home, I'm just singing for myself, it's OK, it's relaxing sometimes. But if I'm actually going to do it ... it's very worrying.' Famously, he doesn't sing live any more, having struggled in the old days with poor sound systems, and all the problems of live amplification, and now perhaps – even though technological improvements would probably have done away with at least some of these issues – simply can't imagine revving himself back up, getting back on that stage, and performing ... well, what? The new stuff or the old stuff? Which Scott would people want to come and see, which voice would they be paying to listen to?

Just imagine, one of those nostalgia gigs, playing the old, beloved album in its entirety on some London stage. Scott performing, but which one – Scott 3? Scott 4? The whole music industry would be there, wouldn't they? Everyone in England who's made a record in the last thirty years. I imagine there's nothing he's less likely to do. I would be there in a shot if he did, and I don't blame him for a second for not wanting to.

21

WE ALL SING

There is a lovely quote from Ann Patchett's *Bel Canto* which is a very simple and sincere description of what listening to singing can feel like. It's one that I find moving and, perhaps more importantly, am comfortable with as an idea: 'Her voice stays inside him, becomes him. She is singing her part to him, and to a thousand other people. He is anonymous, equal, loved.'

What this suggests to me is connection. Not the singer being elevated above the listener, and above the crowd, but becoming as one with the listener, at the same time as the listener is joined to all other listeners. It's about singing as a communal, shared experience – something inevitably human and humble. Perhaps this is more what we want; less of a separation, more of a joining together. A feeling that we are all in it together.

I've been asked: What's it like when you join in at

moments of group singing, for example, 'Happy Birthday', when the cake is brought to the table? Does everyone gradually stop singing, shamed into silence by the presence of your beautiful voice? No, of course not, is the answer, although it is true to say that I have been in situations where I think I can sense people at least looking at me, and wondering, is she going to sound better than us when we all start singing this, or not?

And the truth is, not. No one sounds any better than anybody else when singing 'Happy Birthday', unless you're the kind of idiot who starts doing Mariah Carey trills at the end of each line, and then veers off into a harmony on the chorus, in which case you're going to sound worse than everybody else. There is basically nothing you can do to the tune of 'Happy Birthday' that will demonstrate your singing prowess, and as for doing a Marilyn Monroe impersonation – please, this is not the place.

The only thing I do try to do, whenever a round of 'Happy Birthday' is called for, is to be the one to establish the opening note, because if you leave this to others, someone (a man) will start it too low for everyone, or someone else (a child) will start it in a range that ends in a region only audible to dogs. So I loudly pick a note somewhere central, and hope everyone will join in and it will sound at least reasonable. They never do.

I wish you could do this in church, but of course there you are thwarted by the organist, who is the one picking the note you all start on. I go to my kids' school carol service every year, because it's Christmas and I disapprove of all Scrooge-like behaviour at Christmas, and that includes refusal to sing carols just because they go on about the virgin's womb and the incarnate deity. And I enjoy singing the carols, but the one thing that makes this almost impossible is the keys they are pitched in. Sing with the ladies and it will be assumed you are a soprano, so pretty soon you're warbling away in your flutiest head voice and sounding like the Queen Mother. Join in with the men instead and it's a Barry White impression all the way. I end up doing that awful thing of singing one section in the ladies' octave until it gets way too high for me, at which point I drop to the range below, joining the guys but sounding, in the process, like a thirteen-year-old boy whose voice is breaking. It's humiliating, and anyone standing nearby thinking, This'll be good, I get to hear Tracey Thorn singing 'Adeste Fideles', is in for a major disappointment. The truth is, when singing 'Hark the Herald Angels Sing', I don't sound any better than your nan.

What about karaoke, then? Surely that's an opportunity to shine? To really show off and show them how it's done? Well, I'm no karaoke expert, having done it only once in my life, but in my experience – limited, yes, but accurate nonetheless – karaoke is only ever performed drunk, and we all know how people sing when they're drunk. You've seen that iPhone footage of Kim Wilde on a train after Christmas drinks, performing 'Kids in America' to a startled carriage with a look on her face of someone who has a song in her heart and not a care in the world? It's a magnificent thing, and the only correct response is to love Kim Wilde for it, but the singing? That's how we all sound when we're drunk. All of us.

So when I went on a karaoke evening a couple of years back, with some women friends from Twitter, I soon learned that it wasn't going to be about me seizing the mic at some point and moving everyone to tears with my version of a Leonard Cohen song. No, it was all about Grace Dent's poignant interpretation of 'Wuthering Heights', Sue Perkins's faithful and respectful Scottish accent on the Proclaimers' 'I'm Gonna Be (500 Miles)', and finally, me plucking up the courage to duet on Will Young's 'Leave Right Now' with Radio 4's Alice Arnold, spicing it up with the sudden and unexpected addition of a tambourine solo. Was anyone impressed, or even interested in whether I sounded any good? No, of course not, they were looking round the room to see where they'd put their drink and scrolling through the list of songs to cue up 'Total Eclipse of the Heart'.

Still, communal singing is an activity that we value; it's popular, perhaps more popular again now than it has been for a long time. A hundred years ago it was taken for granted that people sang, in that 'make your own entertainment' kind of way around the piano in pubs, or more seriously every Sunday in church. But as Will Hodgkinson writes in *The Ballad of Britain*, in the twentieth century, with the birth of the music industry, people began to leave music to the professionals: 'The average Briton accepted they were rubbish at singing, as they were at most things in life, and simply stopped doing it.' Recently, however, it seems to me that people have rediscovered how much they enjoy singing, and the growing popularity of secular choirs is evidence of this – as also, perhaps, is the willingness of thousands of people to take part in auditions for shows like *The X Factor*. The show is held up as an example of our passivity – like vegetables we loll in front of the telly, watching the bland and the talentless, music becoming nothing more than aural wallpaper. But this is to ignore the countless numbers who turn up to try and be on the programme, people who clearly don't regard it as an excuse to be passive, but an opportunity to join in, to participate in the business of music, to seize it back from the professionals. Noel Coward quipped that television was for appearing on, not for watching, and via the medium of the talent show it is possible nowadays for the non-celebrity to live up to his maxim.

The popularity of Gareth Malone's TV series *The Choir* is again testament to the fact that people like to take part in communal singing, even if they sometimes do it vicariously by watching others in a choir. Around the country choirs have had a resurgence, suggesting that for many people, singing is more fun to do than to listen to – there is a euphoric experience to be had from the physical sensations of singing as opposed to listening, and an endorphin-releasing element which also informs people's desire to run marathons or leap about at zumba classes. These kinds of choirs have moved away from associations with churches and a strictly classical repertoire and towards working with more mixed material, and a more relaxed approach to the vocal skills of the participants. At this level, taking part brings the joys of a kind of risk-free singing. In a sense, singing in a choir is an example of singing without being heard, even a version of Dusty's 'singing into a void', in that you can't distinctly hear your own voice above those of the group, and equally you can't be heard in an individual sense, you are merely part of the whole. This is a long way from what we think of as choral singing, where discipline is key and every voice counts. In the latter context, as John Potter points out, a chorister is obliged to raise a hand and 'own up' if they make a mistake, so that the choirmaster knows who has faltered; but in the modern, democratic, Gareth Malone-style of choir, it is all about getting everyone to feel confident and worthy. Getting the best out of each singer according to their ability is a more achievable goal than striving to get the best result possible.

At weddings and funerals we still sometimes sing hymns, but often, in these secular times, traditional hymns have given way to other kinds of music and singing that seem to capture the mood. At a funeral this is usually the moment that releases tears, as though the singing voice unlocks something, allows us to acknowledge that we have, in our grief, moved outside the realm of the normal and everyday, with its stiff upper lip and putting on a brave face. Music pushes those formalities aside, expressing the things we haven't been able to say, even in the eulogies we may have written, the condolences we have offered. Ella Fitzgerald sang 'Every Time We Say Goodbye' at the end of the funeral service for my mum, and for Ben's sister recently it was James Taylor singing 'You've Got a Friend'. I won't forget those moments, or be able to hear those songs again without being transported back, but that's OK, we can bear being reminded.

Singing on the dancefloor can be as much a part of the communal club experience as the dancing, which is why

I get frustrated when club music goes through phases of being completely instrumental. The Streets' 'Weak Become Heroes' is Mike Skinner's paean to the nights and days of rave, but in the euphoric landscape he describes, all rising pianos and floating emotions, it's not so much the dancing he remembers – in fact he barely mentions it. What seems to be the emotional core of this song, the proof he offers that in those few moments everyone around him was bonded in a way he had never known before or since, was the fact that 'we all sing, we all sing'. I can't hear that song without a tug of emotion, and not out of nostalgia, for it was a scene I had no part in, but because, unlike anything else that's ever been written about rave culture, this song makes me envious. It's that image of everyone on the dancefloor together, eyes closed, singing. 'Sing to the words, flex to the fat one, the tribal drums, the sun's rising. We all smile. We all sing.' It's a melancholy, elegiac track, so it's no wonder that it's moving – he's talking about feelings he's never been able to recapture – but I love the fact that in trying to encapsulate what was essential about the experience, he settles on the fact that everyone was singing. It immediately conjures up for me other moments, memories or imaginings, when people have sung together, spontaneously, in unrehearsed situations, and it has been something joyous, unpredictable and unifying. Most vividly, it brings to my mind a poem by Siegfried Sassoon, 'Everyone Sang', written about the end of the First World War. You might think that's stretching it a bit – that the euphoria occasioned by the ending of years of slaughter can't really be compared to the dancefloor hedonism of a crowd of pilled-up ravers. But they move me in similar ways.

'Everyone suddenly burst out singing; / And I was filled with such delight / As prisoned birds must find in freedom, [. . .] Everyone's voice was suddenly lifted; / And beauty came like the setting sun: / My heart was shaken with tears; and horror drifted away . . . O, but Everyone / Was a bird; and the song was wordless; the singing will never be done.'

We all sing, and we all sing together and, thankfully, it will never be done.

22

THE EMPTY VESSEL

When we sing communally we tend to go easy on ourselves – we're doing our best, just having a laugh even, don't judge us. But when we listen to an individual singer we set the bar higher, and I don't just mean in terms of technical performance. We're searching for something that isn't merely sound without content, and we strive to distinguish between singing that has something essential and full about it, and singing which is lacking, missing some vital ingredient. A book that explores the possibility that a singer can sometimes be an empty vessel, and coincidentally one of the strangest books I've ever read, is George du Maurier's *Trilby*. You've probably never read it, might not even have heard of it, but let me tell you that, although it is little read now, it was an absolute smash hit in its day. First serialised in the American magazine *Harper's Monthly* in 1894, published as a bestselling novel the following year, then adapted into a hit play and more than one movie, it gave the world both the trilby hat, and the character Svengali – part singing teacher, part mesmerist, who transforms tone-deaf Trilby O'Ferrall into the world's greatest superstar diva. So far, so bizarre.

Svengali is the classic artist manqué – he had longed to be a singer himself, and spent years studying, but nature had been cruel to him – 'He was absolutely without voice, beyond the harsh, weak raven's croak he used to speak with, and no method availed to make one for him.' It is clear, though, that he knows all there is to know about singing, and that in his imagination he is constantly singing, transforming any paltry piece of music into something glorious: 'There was nothing so humble, so base even, but that his magic could transform it into the rarest beauty without altering a note.' The act of singing is defined here as magic, but magic that can only be performed if the basic raw materials, the innate sound of the voice, are in place to begin with, and for Svengali this is not so.

Enter Trilby – boyish, tall, laidback, dressed in a masculine style and smoking her own roll-ups; cheerful on the surface but obviously possessed of dark secrets and repressed feelings. The joke about Trilby – and it is presented at first as a joke – is that she can't sing, despite having an extraordinary-sounding voice – 'a volume of breathy sound, not loud, but so immense that it seemed to come from all round'. We first hear her sing a simple folk tune to some friends, and 'It was as though she could never once have deviated into tune, never once have hit upon a true note, even by a fluke – in fact, as though she were absolutely tone-deaf, and without ear'.

She meets Svengali, who instantly grasps that she has an amazing-*sounding* voice but no musical ear at all. She enjoys singing, yet is ignorant of the mistakes she makes: when Svengali tests her by playing two different notes on the piano, she declares that they are the same. She is tone-deaf but entirely oblivious and without self-consciousness. Singing, then, means almost nothing to her; she can enjoy it as any amateur might, a pure physical pleasure, without depth. His attitude towards her at this point is completely dehumanising. He regards her as an instrument, with the body of a singer, but none of the musical or mental skills necessary. *He* is the artist, she merely his vessel.

Time passes, we lose sight of her, then re-encounter her later in the novel when a group of people are discussing the new singing sensation 'La Svengali', and as each person joins in they try to outdo each other in superlative praise, their flamboyant descriptions of her vocal prowess becoming more and more over-the-top as they go on: 'The voice is a detail. It's what she does with it – it's incredible! It gives one cold all down the back! It drives you mad! It makes you weep hot tears by the spoonful!'

This, we realise, is tone-deaf Trilby they are talking about, and her reinvention as the greatest singer the world has ever known causes du Maurier some descriptive problems, as he runs out of adjectives in trying to describe the unutterable perfection of her singing voice – 'its intonation absolutely, mathematically pure; one felt it to be not only faultless, but infallible ... The like of that voice has never been heard, nor ever will be again. A woman archangel might sing like that, or some enchanted princess out of a fairy tale.' This kind of hyperbole goes on for a full *seven pages*, until by the end, the entire audience at Trilby's concert, which is composed of 'the most cynically critical people in the world' are a sobbing, emotionally drained mess.

But how has this miracle been achieved? Well, by the power of hypnosis. Svengali has mesmerised her and she is performing in a trance, after which she will be unable to recall any of her great moments of performance. Effectively, she is not even present during these feats of singing genius. Svengali is singing through her: *his* is the artistic achievement, but due to an accident of anatomy, he is forced to use her body as a means of production. When Svengali dies, Trilby can no longer sing, and is laughed off stage by an audience who hear her suddenly revert to her old tunelessness.

This, I think, is the frankest example in literature of the dehumanising attitude towards the singer. Nowhere will you find a more complete disconnect between the person and the voice; she has no control over her singing, no stake in it; no part of her personality is present in it. It's partly just a tale of its time, in a similar vein to Shaw's *Pygmalion* – the idea of a male talent taking possession of a vacant, passive female form and animating it in his own fashion, using it to bring to life his own ideals, imposing himself on the world through the body of another, and it's no accident that this other is a woman. Trilby is at first glance an interesting and non-conformist character, but the world damages and denigrates her, and in her reduced state she is left vulnerable and falls prey to the machinations of Svengali, who exploits her for his own purposes, to realise his thwarted artistic ambitions. It is his dreams being fulfilled – and, you could argue, his 'voice' that reduces the audience to tears.

It's an odd tale. Fantastical, improbable, overwritten, mawkish and sentimental much of the time. Melodramatic and repetitive. And yet in the character of Svengali, and his power over Trilby, it has handed down to us a stereotype that we recognise to this day. The manipulative puppet-master, hungrily seeking raw talent – talent that doesn't even know of its own existence, or power, and doesn't know its own desires – and consuming it. The performer as zombie, animated only by the efforts of a behind-the-scenes schemer. Here, in *Trilby*, we have the archetype of that story, so prevalent in discussions of the pop world. You don't need me to say the words Simon Cowell here, do you? Shall we talk about *The X Factor*?

23

THE X FACTOR

I'm not supposed to like *The X Factor*, am I? In fact, I'm not even supposed to watch it, let alone like it. I know this because every Saturday when it's on, people (I say people, I mean men) tell me so on Twitter. That I have shocked and disappointed them. First, someone will say, 'I can't believe you watch this crap! You're a *real* musician, not like this talentless bunch! I'm so disappointed in you! Why don't you turn your TV off and do something creative instead!' And then, whatever the result on a Sunday night, whoever has been voted off – whether by the judges or by public vote – someone will shriek, 'It's a fix! I can't believe you watch this crap, it is such a *fix*!'

So yes, I know and I understand that people don't like it, and that there are valid reasons not to like it. I watch it semi-ironically, same as everyone else, and I enjoy tweeting about it as much as, if not more than, the actual watching and the listening. I'd be lying if I said that I always, or even regularly enjoy it on a purely musical level. Too much of the time, I agree, it is wearying in the extreme. The same three songs that have recently featured in adverts come round again and again. Decades' worth of well-loved and eminently coverable songs sit neglected on a dusty warehouse shelf somewhere, tumbleweed blowing down the aisles, while the contestants are asked yet again to choose between 'What a Wonderful World' or something by Queen. I remember the week barmaid Sophie Habibis sang 'Bang Bang (My Baby Shot Me Down)' by Sonny Bono, a rare example of a genuinely interesting and unexpected song choice. This was more like it, I thought. A different song, familiar to some of us but not all, bringing with it a gentle haze of nostalgia, a whiff of unsullied 1960s innocence. It seemed a perfectly reasonable choice, too – the song is hooky and yet not worn threadbare by repeated revisits. Her rendition wasn't perfect, but no matter – for a brief moment it was as though a door had opened at the back of the stage, and given us a glimpse of the World of Song that lives out there. Tantalising. Full of promise. A kind of ideal of how the show could be, *should* be.

She got voted off.

There is also all too frequently the feeling that we see the best of contestants at the audition stage. That unlike, say, *Strictly Come Dancing*, where there is a genuine all-round improvement in the abilities of most of the contestants as training and weekly performances kick in, on *The X Factor* there is, sadly, a sense that the raw talent which can burst out and surprise you on the audition stage is gradually squeezed into a small and often wrongly shaped box, the corners of which are then remorselessly filed off week by week, till what you're left with is something bland, safe, indistinguishable from things you've seen and heard before many, many times; all sense of individuality, personality, quirk or charm utterly gone.

I agree with people who say that the show can be cruel – I don't enjoy the parade of the more 'vulnerable' contestants at some of the auditions. Even after that stage, when we're down to the finalists, it is of course a lions' den that they are all walking into. In many ways it's a microcosm of the lions' den that is the music industry, and in a single series contestants experience a kind of speeded-up version of a career in music (or at least, a historical version of a career in music) – the audition is the moment when you present your demo tape to an A and R man, judges' houses is the moment when you get signed, and each week in the live finals you perform your new single on *Top of the Pops*, and see how the public responds; do they buy it or not, do you go up the chart or down?

So in many ways, it's no more cruel or unfair than any attempt to make a career in music. You'll be judged not just on the sound of your voice, but on what you look like, how you move – or not – on stage, and what the public perceive you to be like. Do you have what Louis calls 'the likeability factor'? You might be able to sing in tune, but does anybody *want* to hear you sing?

So with all these negatives laid out before us, why do I say I like it? I'll tell you why. It's because, unlike those fans of mine who regularly tweet me to tell me I am better than this show and shouldn't watch it, I don't think I am, or that anybody else in music is better than these hopefuls, these brave souls. And at the moment when they have the mic put in their hand, and the stage manager does that phoney '3-2-1' countdown and pushes them into the limelight, I feel a kinship with them. We are the same, in that moment. I know what it is to have the mic in your hand, and step out onto the unforgiving stage, in the glare of those lights. You don't really know what awaits you out there, certainly not at the start of your career, and it takes a particular and gut-wrenching courage. They are beginners, mostly, and painfully young. Bright-eyed dreamers, innocents, children, about to venture into a world of weary adult cynics. And the step they take is only one small step, but a giant leap in terms of where they've come from. Some have done gigs before, usually small ones; some have only ever sung in their bedroom; others have toiled for years on the unforgiving circuit of clubs, wine bars, hotel foyers, and this represents their last, their only chance at something bigger. And so they step out onto a huge, slippery stage, in front of not just the live audience but a huge TV audience as well, sometimes also expected to perform a choreographed dance routine, in full costume, for the first time in their lives. My heart is in my throat, and I feel for them, each and every one, each and every time.

'But is it really about singing at all?' you ask. And it's a fair point.

On one simple level, it is Saturday night light entertainment, a version of the good old-fashioned mixed-bag, end-of-the-pier British variety show which has been a mainstay of lazy weekend telly for decades. Understanding it on this level seems to me to go some way to puncturing the earnest, pompous attacks levelled at it by 'music lovers'. It is singing presented as fun, or as a kind of circus, but also, in some strange and unexpected ways, it harks back to a golden age of pop music.

In the early rounds especially, what we are revelling in is the celebration of the amateur, the outsider figure, which is a long-standing and noble tradition within the British pop scene. Characters who look like plasterers and chimney sweeps (as they will prove at interview to actually *be*) will appear with their British teeth and their hairstyles and hats, and act out a potted history of British pop music – which consists of flashes of vocal brilliance and personality, punctuated by some capering clown taking to the stage and demanding his moment in the spotlight.

From the high emotion of some of the performances, through the tawdry sentimentalism of others, right down to the buffoonery of what we might cruelly call the 'joke' acts, it reminds me of what the charts used to be like. Diana Ross next to Wizard. 'American Pie' next to Convoy. Great artists rubbing shoulders with one-hit wonders. Pop music in all its glory.

And this is why I refuse to get angry about the voting for the 'joke' acts, when it happens. There is often fury at this point, when an 'unworthy' contestant scrapes through at the expense of someone apparently better, though what this means is that someone who has entertained you gets more votes than someone who has proved capable of singing in tune, but otherwise has nothing to distinguish them from anyone else who can sing in tune. The fun, silly act trumps the boring, bland one, just like in the real world of pop music.

In pop music the distinction between the amateur and the professional is an arbitrary one. There is no official training to undergo, no moment when you become fully qualified, when you can be called a 'proper' singer. Pop singers are simply people who get up and do it. If they're good at it, and can make a living from it, and become experienced at recording and singing live, then we regard them as professionals. If they become extremely successful, they are stars, and can come to seem distant and unattainable – which is why we then yearn to see 'amateurs' again.

I think that is the key. They are given mentors who are supposed to guide them through the weeks, and the makeovers and the singing lessons are meant to mould them into something akin to a potential pop star. But the outcome is always the same. As they get 'better', they get worse. In the search for the intangible 'X Factor', or the attempt to manufacture it, any hint that might have been present in their early appearances of character, style or individuality is ruthlessly removed.

What we are doing when we watch *The X Factor* is watching ourselves. Those untrained singers who take to the floor, they are us. It could be me, you might think – or even, it doesn't have to be me, I can watch you doing it for me. So singing, once again, is both the great leveller and the embodiment of our yearning for transcendence. They sing as us, often not much better than us; they *are* us. We watch them go on a journey and again, they are going on the journey so that we don't have to. Often, it's quite a disappointing journey. We think we want to go there, but look, it's not much fun really, is it, when you look closely?

It's the blend of the high and the low, the silly and the serious, and yes, the good and the awful, that makes the show, for me. I know there's a point, usually about halfway through, when the joke act has to go, and I accept it but I miss them. Then comes the inexorable last run towards Christmas, with everyone starting to take it all too seriously. Even the singers you liked at the beginning you're now starting to hate because, let's face it, not many of us want to watch even the singers we love most in the world every Saturday night, doing a cover version of a song we don't much like, live on TV. It's too much pressure for any of them to withstand. We reach the end drained and wretched, wondering why we started watching and how this person came to win, out of all that *promise* at the start, and we vow never to watch again. And then we do. I do. I absolutely do.

24

WHY SING?

We can't end there, though, with me watching *The X Factor*. You'd never forgive me, would you, dear reader? I think I know where this has to end, and it's with myself, once again; here with my questions about singing and not singing. Wondering whether I will ever sing on a stage in front of people again. Wondering whether or not I can call myself A Singer if I don't do that any more, and if it matters at all what I call myself, or what anyone else calls me. Wondering *why* we sing at all.

In The Smiths' song 'Asleep', when Morrissey pleads for a lullaby, he seems to be singing about singing, though the overarching theme he is more than hinting at is suicide; the desire not to wake up standing in for a more permanent oblivion, the final everlasting sleep, both seductive and dangerous. But it's the presence of singing at this most crucial turning point, or ending point, of a life that catches my attention. The lyrics describe his subject's yearning for someone to sing to him, his longing not to wake up on his own, and they suggest that we're never truly alone as long as someone is singing to us. A voice is there, even as we drift into unconsciousness – whether of sleep or death – and that singing voice is as tangibly comforting as a hand softly caressing our hair, a blanket placed over our weary body. Don't hold me, don't just talk to me, but sing. It means so much.

In Keats' 'Ode to a Nightingale', the bird's song is immortal, yet speaks to the poet's longing for death. Like Morrissey, Keats seems to feel that one would not die alone if someone, or something – in this case a bird – were singing at that moment: 'Now more than ever seems it rich to die, / To cease upon the midnight with no pain, / While thou art pouring forth thy soul abroad / In such an ecstasy!' Birdsong equals freedom, a release from the cares and pains of existence; and the song's ecstasy is soothing, an accompaniment to life or death which takes away the suffering, or at least makes it bearable. How often we seem to return to the idea that song can ease us from this life, transport our souls to heaven, gently carry us from this world to the next: 'And flights of angels sing thee to thy rest!' (*Hamlet*).

We sing to make ourselves feel better, and we sing for others to make them feel better. In this book, I've focused on the trouble with being a singer, in an attempt to balance out some of the idealised cliches I've grown tired of. And I've looked for stories that mirror my own, and for singers who feel, or have felt, like me. But that doesn't mean I think it's all bad, or that we're all mad, all the time. Take Alison Moyet, for instance. Over the years she has become somewhat saddled with an image which is almost a stereotypical portrait of the artist as a bit of a nutcase. Recent interviews and press articles have seemed to dwell endlessly on her struggles and her demons. When she appeared on *Desert Island Discs* various newspapers ran short pieces about her, pulling out quotes about her agoraphobia, her smashing of her gold discs, constructing a somewhat pained and painful persona: The Damaged Singer.

Alison would be the last to deny the troubles which have beset her career (many of them related to dealings with record companies and contracts) and the psychological problems which accompanied them, but in many ways she is the complete opposite of the tortured artist; someone who has at times been a tortured *person*, but for whom singing has always been the escape; not the source of her fears, but the solution to them. Talking to her, I realise that she is the living embodiment of one valid answer to the question, why sing? She's one of those people for whom singing is actually easier than speaking; it's more true, and more liberating.

She describes herself very frankly as being socially phobic: 'I was always quite insular, I was a bit of a loner ... and then when I got into this business where everyone was sociable, I was just a bit freaked out by it. I got great invites to go to great places, work with brilliant people, you know, do some amazing collaborations, but the terror of meeting people was always enough for me to turn them down.'

*

ME: So for you it was not so much musical- or singing-based fear, it was more social.

ALISON: Yeah, social fear.

ME: Whereas for me it's about the actual singing.

ALISON: Yeah, bizarrely that was the one thing I'm secure about.

ME: See, that's interesting to me. I've talked to a couple of other people who are more like me, who share all my anxieties and angst about singing, and it's all focused on the performing; but you're different.

ALISON: Yeah, I'm very hard on myself, and I have anxieties elsewhere, but the singing is the safe place for me.

ME: So, at gigs, do you feel anxious?

ALISON: No, on stage I'm fine, I know what's expected of me.

ME: And do you need an audience? Do you thrive on the crowd in front of you?

ALISON: No ... I just find fewer people more intimidating than many. And you can't really see the people anyway. You know, I just kind of lose myself in it.

*

More comfortable on stage than most of the other singers I've talked about or spoken to, she is also more rational – less *mad*, if you like – in her ability to judge herself and her own abilities. Not for her Dusty's 'I have a voice I don't particularly like', or Sandy's 'You'll just have to put up with this'. Instead she has a core of steel, forged during the years when things went wrong for her, and she learned how painful shutting herself off from the world could be. Now she has an almost fierce determination never to let that happen again.

ALISON: I'm not really frightened of making mistakes. What I am frightened of is not engaging, because so many of my years were spent avoiding engaging. I am frightened of *not* finding out what I can do. I'm not frightened of finding out what I do badly. And maybe I say that because I know that when I do things well I do them really well. And maybe it's because I come with that confidence. But I can hear my brilliance, and I can hear my idiocy. My complete failings.

ME: You have the most clear-sighted vision of yourself as a singer. More so than anyone else I've talked to.

ALISON: Really?

ME: Haha, yes, you're the most level-headed of all of us. You win! And I know you think of yourself as someone who's full of angst and everything—

ALISON: Oh I am, though, I am full of angst.

ME: Yes, but in terms of your persona as a singer, you win the crown for being sorted and sussed.

ALISON: Hoorah!

Talking to Alison is inspiring, but it also can't help but make me aware of the gap between us, the different arenas in which our neuroses play out. I wanted to include her as a positive voice, but her take on singing doesn't really coincide with mine. We all have our own reasons, our own motivations for singing, and it fulfils different needs or plays on different fears in each of us. For some, singing can be a form of showing off, done to impress; after all, the voice can be a seductive instrument. I was conscious quite early on that my voice was considered to have a sexy quality, being low-pitched, warm, a little breathy. This was interesting for me, as I had never considered myself sexy. I wasn't a conventionally pretty teenager; I didn't meet the mainstream ideal, so I had doubted my appeal. But then the voice seemed to do it for me, and gave me access to a power I hadn't had before. And yet, still, there was the conundrum – was it *me* listeners were attracted to, or the disembodied voice? If it was seductive, who was doing the seducing? If someone swooned while listening to a record, I wasn't even present, so it was hard to see how I was involved in the frisson being experienced. It was as though I poured something into a sealed bottle – a love potion! – which was then opened when I wasn't in the room, and worked its effects.

But how I benefited from those effects was not an easy question to answer.

Set against this egotistical aspect of singing, which exploits the possibility of personal allure, is the concept of singing as a shared experience, something to join us together. Singing can be empowering for an individual, yet at the same time there's a democracy to it. You may say you 'can't sing', but I bet you can sing more than you can play guitar, or do a drum solo. So you have a stake in it. When you listen to singers, you're listening to people doing something you've done yourself, something you've shared in. So the communal, joining together element is there, even when we listen to singers. And when we take part in singing with others, then it becomes literally communal – the sharing of an experience in real time. If we sing at least in part to express our inner selves and our feelings, then perhaps doing so with others amplifies that aspect of emotional self-expression. Our feelings, whatever they may be – joy, despair, passion – join together with those of the other singers, and we're bonded by the act, the taking part.

The folk singers Rachel and Becky Unthank have started in recent years to host what they call 'Singing Weekends', where a group of people take part in singing workshops, communal harmony sessions, a sing-song in the pub – various forms of singing together in a non-professional capacity, for the simple pleasure of joining in. The idea sounded both intriguing and attractive to me, so I decided that I would like to attend one in order both to observe and to take part in this type of communal singing. Booking my attendance with Adrian, Rachel's husband, I explained to him that I was writing this book, and mentioned that I'd like to include something about the singing weekends in it. He was happy with this, and so I planned to set off for Berwick-upon-Tweed in January 2014.

Anticipating the singing weekend I was about to attend, I began in my mind to build it up into something possibly life-changing, imagining that I might have a kind of epiphany; a moment when I would find myself singing with a crowd of strangers and rediscover the joy of singing out loud in public. I even had the idea that it could provide me with the final trajectory of this book – that all my doubts and questioning would be resolved in some way in this concluding chapter, which would answer some of those questions and provide me with a point of closure.

But as the day I was due to go drew nearer, I realised I was experiencing serious anxieties about it; beginning to dread it, even, fearing that it wouldn't be what I'd built it up to be – and could in fact be a disaster. That, however much I loved and respected the notion of communal singing, of everyone being equal in a group setting, I was too far gone down the path of being a Professional Singer to easily shed that identity, or expect others to let me shed it. I feared that everyone would in fact look at me, expect something from me, *want* something from me, and that it might actually be even worse than being on stage, in that we would be up close, eyeball to eyeball, and there would be no escape.

Far from looking forward to confronting my issues around singing, I had to acknowledge that I was no nearer being able to do that than I had been for the last fifteen years or more. Suffering from a winter cold, I worried that I wouldn't even be able to sing, and so a day or two before the weekend, I cancelled. What *was* this, I wondered? Was my body trying to tell me something? Had I deliberately, if subconsciously, sabotaged my attempt to sing again? And in fact, was I still just burying my head in the sand by asking this weekend to be a kind of quick fix, like the failed hypnotherapy – an intervention that would provide a solution to something I had unnecessarily identified as being a problem?

Perhaps, it occurred to me, I was even being slightly dishonest, in that I was trying to *make* something happen which I was then going to present as a bolt from the blue, a moment when I would be thunderstruck by my rekindled love of singing to people. Was there a danger, I wondered, that I was trying to turn this book into a self-help book, involving me 'going on a journey' and 'finding myself' at the end? That hadn't been my original intention, and wasn't what I wanted. And so, with a somewhat heavy heart, I accepted that my neat ending wasn't going to be provided by a weekend of communal singing – which left me, momentarily, looking at an empty space, a blank page where I had thought my conclusion was going to be.

Here we are, though, with the end fast approaching, neat or not. This book hasn't been a journey, nor, I realise, have I wanted it to be; rather, it's given me an opportunity to think and talk about singing in more detail than I had room for in *Bedsit Disco Queen*. There's no chronology here, so no obvious place to end, and I've asked more questions than I've been able to provide answers for; but in exploring my problems with singing, and identifying with other singers who've experienced similar feelings, I realise that I have ended up not far from where I started, back with the notion of singing but not being overheard. I briefly wanted this book to contain a sense of a straight line, of an arrow going somewhere, of progress being made. My last book ended with me apparently reaching a point of acceptance of my place within music, realising that I no longer had anything to prove, that I could finally be myself.

Well, that may be true, and in many important respects I do feel exactly that. But one thing remains – though I have returned to writing and recording songs, I still haven't sung on a stage since the year 2000, at a concert in Montreux. What I don't want to do, however, is carry on implying that this is a great failure on my part. If I'm not going to conclude with a triumphant moment of return, then I am at least going to allow myself the luxury of an ending where I defend my choice, and forgive myself.

Because I of all people, with my love of privacy and my lifelong adherence to quietness, should be able to admit that there are times when singing can exist for its own sake, with no goal in mind, not even any listener to please. As I've said before, sometimes the best moment during the making of a record is the point when you are just beginning to write the songs, and they exist solely inside your head; you have tunes and bits of lyrics that only you have heard. You sing them, aloud and to yourself, and it's a completely private activity. Equally, sometimes it can be enough to sing for the sake of making a lovely sound, pure and simple, no need for any instrument, just your own body producing a noise. I've always found this pleasurable. Having started out making music in solitude, preferring not to be witnessed, sealing myself off wherever possible from any listener, I would find satisfaction in the creation of sound that only I experienced. And I still enjoy doing this. One of my daughters shares this impulse with me. She goes down into our soundproofed basement studio, plays the piano and sings to herself, and no one is allowed to listen. She doesn't like performing, doesn't like being watched, doesn't much need or want anyone else's opinion or approval. She's not trying to entertain, or prove a point, or achieve anything. They are her own private moments of self-expression.

This is the opposite of what I have said about the communal aspect of singing. It might seem at odds with it; too insular – selfish, even – almost a waste, to create something and not share it. But it doesn't feel like that to me. Solitary activity is sometimes devalued in our gregarious, extrovert-friendly culture. We admire those who are confident and social, and worry about or even patronise those who are introverted or shy. You can be labelled a loser for spending too much time in your bedroom, playing computer games or having online friends, as though experiences which take place outside the home, in the 'real world', are inherently richer, more rewarding, more valuable. And is the same true of music? Do we assume that making music in public is a more worthwhile thing to do than singing at home, in private, to ourselves? If I write a song, or sing someone else's, does it only count if I then record it and sell it to you, or get on a stage and sing it to you from up there?

Maybe, after all, this is the epiphany of my book. Not a change of heart, or an uplifting moment when I overcome the barriers that have stood in my way, shoving them aside as I stride back onto the stage, a new woman. But instead a moment when I stop beating myself up. When I acknowledge, as I have since reading Susan Cain's book *Quiet*, that I am a classic introvert, who just happened to be born with a singing voice, but for whom the stage has always been more or less a scene of torment; and, most importantly, that this need not be a source of guilt or shame.

For when I say I 'don't sing', that isn't really what I mean. In actual fact, I *do* sing, it's just that quite often, like the proverbial tree falling in the forest, there is no one there to hear me. But *I* hear me. I feel the breath go in and out of my body, I relish the sensation of doing something I know how to do, I feel in possession and in control of an ability that's long been there for me. I've spent a lot of time singing for others, and much of the time I've enjoyed it; I value the moments when I have music to share, new songs to record, and I'm certainly not going to stop doing that. And as much as I agonise over whether or not I should go on tour again, or appear on telly, or sing live on the radio, much of the time I simply don't think about it at all, and it doesn't seem to matter whether or not I ever do any of those things again. Sometimes, I sing just for the sake of it; because I can, and because I want to.

I just sing.

ACKNOWLEDGEMENTS

I would like to give huge thanks:

to my agent Kirsty McLachlan, who read the book in its very early stages and made extremely useful comments

to Ben Watt, who also read it at an early stage, putting 'HAHA' in the margin at intervals, which was encouraging, and who pointed out that I needed a snappy title

to Rowan Cope, my editor at Virago, who read it in the later stages, and whose invaluable help and suggestions enabled me to finish

to Zoë Hood and Emily Burns at Virago for all their unstinting work on the publicity side of things

to Romy Madley Croft, Green Gartside, Alison Moyet, Kristin Hersh and Linda Thompson for agreeing to answer my questions about singing

and to Amber Burlinson, who copy-edited the whole thing with an eye for detail which I take my hat off to. To which I take my hat off? Oh, I'm not sure – that's why I needed her.

BIBLIOGRAPHY

I'm indebted to several books for inspiration and extraordinary insights into singing, in particular:

Ian Bostridge *A Singer's Notebook* (Faber & Faber, 2011)
Simon Frith *Performing Rites: On the Value of Popular Music* (Oxford University Press, 1998)
Clinton Heylin *No More Sad Refrains: The Life and Times of Sandy Denny* (Helter Skelter, 2000)
Lenny Kaye *You Call It Madness: The Sensuous Song of the Croon* (Villard Books, 2004)
Wayne Koestenbaum *The Queen's Throat: Opera, Homosexuality, and the Mystery of Desire* (Da Capo Press, 2001)
Lucy O'Brien *Dusty* (Sidgwick & Jackson, 1988)
John Potter *Vocal Authority: Singing Style and Ideology* (Cambridge University Press, 1998)
Randy L. Schmidt *Little Girl Blue: The Life of Karen Carpenter* (Omnibus Press, 2012)

Others that have been useful include:

Margaret Atwood 'Siren Song' *Selected Poems 1965–75* (Virago Press, 1976)

Charlotte Brontë *Shirley* (1849)

Willa Cather *The Song of the Lark* (Virago Press, 1982)

John Cheever *The Wapshot Scandal* (Vintage Classics, 2010)

George du Maurier *Trilby* (1895)

Bob Dylan *Chronicles Volume One* (Simon & Schuster, 2004)

George Eliot *Daniel Deronda* (1876)

Lavinia Greenlaw *The Importance of Music to Girls* (Faber & Faber, 2007)

Kristin Hersh *Paradoxical Undressing* (Penguin, 2010; Atlantic Books 2011)

Will Hodgkinson *The Ballad of Britain: How Music Captured the Soul of a Nation* (Portico, 2009)

James Joyce *Ulysses* (1922)

Franz Kafka 'The Silence of the Sirens' *The Complete Short Stories* (Vintage Classics, 1992)

Gareth Malone *Choir* (Collins, 2012)

Greg Milner *Perfecting Sound Forever: The Story of Recorded Music* (Granta Books, 2009)

Ann Patchett *Bel Canto* (Fourth Estate, 2001)

Arthur Phillips *The Song Is You* (Duckworth Overlook, 2009)

Oliver Sacks *Musicophilia* (Vintage, 2008)

Siegfried Sassoon 'Everyone Sang' *Collected Poems 1908–56* (Faber & Faber, 1961)

Donna Soto-Morettini *Popular Singing* (A&C Black, 2006)

Anne Tyler *A Slipping-Down Life* (Hamlyn, 1983)
Rob Young *Electric Eden: Unearthing Britain's Visionary Music* (Faber & Faber, 2010)
Edited by Rob Young *No Regrets: Writings on Scott Walker* (Orion, 2012)

Interviews and features:

Jonathan Amos 'Girls also have angelic voices' (http://news.bbc.co.uk, 8 September 2003)
Simon Hattenstone 'Scott Walker: Brother Beyond' (*Guardian*, 23 November 2012)
Rob Jones '8 Voices of Bob Dylan' (http://thedelete-bin.com, 24 May 2010)
Jonathan Law 'Disappearing Acts: Shelagh McDonald' (http://thedabbler.co.uk, 6 March 2013)
Rebecca Morelle 'Choir boys' and girls' distinctive voices studied' (http://www.bbc.co.uk, 6 January 2011)
Alexis Petridis 'Gone but not forgotten', interview with Anne Briggs (*Guardian*, 3 August 2007)
Jude Rogers 'You want no sheen, just the song', interview with Shirley Collins (*Guardian*, 21 March 2008)
Graeme Thomson 'Anne Briggs at 65' (http://ishotaman-inrenobook.blogspot.com, 15 August 2008)

SONG CREDITS

PLAYLIST

This is a playlist containing most of the singers mentioned in this book, plus a few I missed. Some of these performances are only included because of their relevance to a particular chapter, but many of them are my favourite vocals of all time. I've listed them in the order in which they appear, and then added more – and quite frankly, I could have gone on for ever.

Patti Smith 'Gloria', 'Kimberly'
Bob Dylan 'Corrina, Corrina'
Elvis Costello 'Alison'
Nico 'The Fairest of the Seasons'
Bridget St John 'Autumn Lullaby'
Oasis 'Supersonic'
Randy Newman 'In Germany Before the War'
Björk 'Human Behaviour'
Elvis Costello 'I Just Don't Know What to Do with
       Myself'
Dusty Springfield 'I Don't Want to Hear it Any More',
       'Nothing Has Been Proved', 'Easy Evil'

Aretha Franklin 'I Say a Little Prayer'
Whitney Houston 'Saving All My Love for You'
Kristin Hersh 'Your Ghost'
Tom Waits 'Martha'
Lou Reed 'Coney Island Baby'
Sex Pistols 'Pretty Vacant'
X-Ray Spex 'The Day the World Turned Day-Glo'
The Fall 'The Container Drivers'
Siouxsie and the Banshees 'Love in a Void'
Marianne Faithfull 'The Ballad of Lucy Jordan'
Au Pairs 'Repetition', 'Headache for Michelle'
Billie Holiday 'I Cover the Waterfront'
The Carpenters 'We've Only Just Begun', 'Goodbye to
    Love', 'Rainy Days and Mondays'
Elvis Costello 'She', '(The Angels Wanna Wear My) Red
    Shoes'
Felt 'Penelope Tree'
Tammy Wynette 'I Don't Wanna Play House'
Massive Attack 'Karmacoma'
Molly Drake 'How Wild the Wind Blows'
The Rolling Stones 'Angie'
Ray Charles 'You Don't Know Me'
Nat King Cole 'Stardust'
Elton John 'Tiny Dancer'
David Bowie 'The Jean Genie', 'Letter to Hermione'
Roxy Music 'Virginia Plain'
Scritti Politti 'Confidence', 'The Sweetest Girl'
The Beach Boys 'The Warmth of the Sun'
Robert Wyatt 'Born Again Cretin'
Captain Beefheart 'Observatory Crest'

Joni Mitchell 'The Last Time I Saw Richard'
Simon and Garfunkel 'The 59th Street Bridge Song'
Colin Blunstone 'I Don't Believe in Miracles'
Bob Dylan 'Talkin' New York'
Nick Drake 'Poor Boy'
John Martyn 'Go Down Easy'
Rachel Unthank and The Winterset 'Felton Lonnin'
Anne Briggs 'Standing on the Shore'
Aretha Franklin 'I'm In Love'
Luther Vandross 'A House Is Not a Home'
Sade 'By Your Side'
The Pretenders 'Talk of the Town'
Blossom Dearie 'May I Come In?'
Björk 'Hyperballad'
Adele 'Make You Feel My Love'
Loleatta Holloway 'Love Sensation'
Beyoncé 'If I Were a Boy'
Marni Nixon 'I Feel Pretty'
Daft Punk 'One More Time'
Poliça 'Dark Star'
Rufus Wainwright 'Memphis Skyline'
Ben Watt 'Matthew Arnold's Field'
Barbra Streisand 'Stoney End'
Frank Sinatra 'Love Is Here to Stay'
Velvet Underground 'Sunday Morning'
The xx 'Night Time'
Fleetwood Mac 'Dreams'
Wings 'My Love'
Jessie Ware 'Running'
This Mortal Coil 'Song to the Siren'

Vashti Bunyan 'Diamond Day'
Shelagh McDonald 'Let No Man Steal Your Thyme'
Linda Thompson 'Dimming of the Day'
Anne Briggs 'Sovay'
The Mamas and the Papas 'Dream a Little Dream of Me'
Michael Jackson 'Got to Be There' (acapella)
Fairport Convention 'Who Knows Where the Time
     Goes?', 'Autopsy'
Sandy Denny 'Next Time Around'
Fotheringay 'Silver Threads and Golden Needles'
Joni Mitchell 'Don't Interrupt the Sorrow'
Frank Sinatra 'In the Wee Small Hours of the Morning'
Rod Stewart 'You Wear it Well'
Rufus Wainwright 'Dinner at Eight'
Rudy Vallée 'The Way You Look Tonight'
Chet Baker 'I Get Along Without You Very Well'
American Music Club 'Why Won't You Stay'
Paul Buchanan 'My True Country'
David Sylvian 'Orpheus'
Elbow 'The Night Will Always Win'
Radiohead 'House of Cards'
Scott Walker 'Only Myself to Blame', 'The World's
     Strongest Man', 'Angels of Ashes'
Ella Fitzgerald 'Every Time We Say Goodbye'
James Taylor 'You've Got a Friend'
The Streets 'Weak Become Heroes'
Cher 'Bang Bang (My Baby Shot Me Down)'
Jeff Buckley 'Everybody Here Wants You'
Cocteau Twins 'Musette and Drums'
Mary Margaret O'Hara 'Year in Song'

The Ronettes 'Walking in the Rain'
The Shangri-Las 'I Can Never Go Home Any More'
Judee Sill 'The Kiss'
Donny Hathaway 'Love, Love, Love'
Sam Cooke 'You Send Me'
Michael McDonald 'I Can Let Go Now'
Stevie Wonder 'Think of Me as Your Soldier'
A Girl Called Eddy 'Somebody Hurt You'
Elastica 'Waking Up'
Feist 'Inside and Out'
Beth Gibbons 'Mysteries'
Judy Collins 'Both Sides Now'
Dolly Parton 'Here You Come Again'
Judy Garland 'Life Is Just a Bowl of Cherries'
Peggy Lee 'The Folks Who Live on the Hill'